SALMA @ Mr

Other McGraw-Hill Books in Mini and Mainframe Computing

ISBN	AUTHOR	TITLE
0-07-056578-3	Sherman	*The CD-ROM Handbook*
0-07-039006-1	Lusardi (hardcover)	*Database Experts' Guide to SQL*
0-07-039002-9	(softcover)	
0-07-016609-6	DeVita (hardcover)	*Database Experts' Guide to FOCUS*
0-07-016604-8	(softcover)	
0-07-036488-5	Larson (hardcover)	*Database Experts' Guide to Database 2*
0-07-023267-9	(softcover)	
0-07-000474-9	Adrian	*The Workstation Data Link*
0-07-057336-0	Simpson, Casey	*Developing Effective User Documentation*
0-07-007248-5	Brathwaite	*Analysis, Design, and Implementation of Data Dictionaries*
0-07-035119-8	Knightson	*Standards for Open Systems Interconnection*
0-07-044938-4	McClain (hardcover)	*VM and Departmental Computing*
0-07-044939-2	(softcover)	
0-07-046302-6	Nemzow	*Keeping the Link*
0-07-038006-6	Lipton	*User Guide to FOCUS™*
0-07-057296-8	Simon	*How to Be a Successful Computer Consultant*
0-07-016188-7	Dayton (Ranade, Ed.)	*Integrating Digital Services*
0-07-002673-4	Azevedo (Ranade Series)	*ISPF: The Strategic Dialog Manager*
0-07-050054-1	Piggott (Ranade Series)	*CICS: A Practical Guide to System Fine Tuning*
0-07-043152-3	Morgan, McGilton	*Introducing UNIX™ System V*
0-07-050686-8	Prasad (Ranade Series)	*IBM Mainframes*
0-07-065087-X	Towner (Ranade Series)	*IDMS/R Cookbook*
0-07-062879-3	Tare (hardcover)	*UNIX™ Utilities*
0-07-062884-X	(softcover)	
0-07-045001-3	McGilton, Morgan	*Introducing the UNIX™ System*
0-07-029750-9	Hood (hardcover)	*Using AutoCAD™ with AutoLISP™*
0-07-029749-5	(softcover)	

AutoCAD™ in 3D

Frank J. Johnson

McGraw-Hill, Inc.

New York   St. Louis   San Francisco   Auckland   Bogotá
Caracas   Hamburg   Lisbon   London   Madrid
Mexico   Milan   Montreal   New Delhi   Paris
San Juan   São Paulo   Singapore
Sydney   Tokyo   Toronto

AUTOCAD™ IN 3D

International Editions 1992

Exclusive rights by McGraw Hill Book Co-Singapore for manufacture and export. This book cannot be re-exported from the country to which it is consigned by McGraw Hill

1 2 3 4 5 6 7 8 9 0 JJP FC 9 6 5 4 3 2

ISBN 0-07-032645-2

Library of Congress Cataloging-in Publication Data

Johnson, Frank J., date
    AutoCAD in 3D / Frank J. Johnson
        p.   cm.
    Includes index.
    ISBN 0-07-032645-2
    1. AutoCAD (Computer program) I. Title.
T385.J63 1991
620'.00425'02855369—dc20   90-42675

The sponsoring editor for this book was Theron Shreve, the editing supervisor was Stephen M. Smith, the designer was Naomi Auerbach, and the production supervisor was Suzanne W. Babeuf.

AutoCAD, AutoSHADE, AutoLISP, AutoFLIX, and AutoSOLID are registered trademarks of Autodesk, Inc.; IBM PC/XT/AT and IBM PS/2, of the international Business Machines Corporation; Ventura Publisher, of Ventura Software, Inc.; MS DOS and OS/2, of Microsoft Corporation.

Certain material in this book was reprinted, with permission, from the *AutoCAD Reference Manual.* Copyright 1988, Autodesk, Inc. Certain material in Chap. 6 was revised and reprinted, with permission, from the AutoCAD 3D Book. Copyright 1989, Ventana Press.

Not for re-sale in Australia, Canada, Europe, Japan, the United Kingdom and the United States Export Sales may be made only by or with expressed consent of the Publisher.

When ordering this title, use ISBN No 0-07-112653-8

Printed in Singapore.

To Fanny and Ed with all my love

Contents

Preface

AutoCAD* is a powerful and easy-to-use computer-aided design and drafting software program. It is the world's best-selling personal-computer-based CAD software package and its sales continue to grow at an astounding rate. It is now considered the industry standard for PC CAD users.

It has become apparent in the CAD industry that a need for designing in three dimensions exists; therefore, Autodesk has developed AutoCAD Releases 10 and 11 with true 3D capabilities. Designing models in three-dimensional space will allow almost any project to be managed more effectively. Such an ability can be applied to almost all AutoCAD professions, including architecture, electrical engineering, chemical engineering, mechanical engineering, civil engineering, interior design, and manufacturing.

Engineers are now able to design computer-generated prototypes to check sizes, fits, and tolerances, and architects will be able to draw 3D floor plans and renderings and have their clients view them from any angle, even from the inside. This will save the designer from building a prototype and save the architect from drawing several sketches of a house, each from a different angle. The surfaces of the 3D drawings can even be shaded to give a rendered effect.

AutoCAD in 3D is an easy-to-read, step-by-step approach to visualizing and effectively designing and drawing 3D models, with documented illustrations to facilitate understanding. Its Introduction describes 3D modeling and its applications and software and hardware requirements, and explains how to use the book. The rest of the book then helps to make the transition from the old way of designing 3D models with AutoCAD to the new way with AutoCAD Release 10: It details all of AutoCAD's new commands to generate and view models in 3D. It teaches how to draw on separate planes in space with AutoCAD's new User Coordinate Systems, design with thickness or height to build 3D wireframe models, create solid surfaces or faces and 3D meshes, and use AutoCAD's multiple viewports and dynamic viewing capabilities. It also illustrates in detail how to use the AutoSHADE program to shade surfaces of a model.

---

* AutoCAD is a registered trademark of Autodesk, Inc.

ACKNOWLEDGMENTS

I would like to thank the following people for their help with the book: The staff at Autodesk, Inc., for its support and for making AutoCAD the powerful 3D drawing tool that it is; the editorial staff at **Cadence** magazine, for the use of some of the material about plotting in 3D contained in Chap. 8; Ventana Press, for permission to use material from its **AutoCAD 3D Book**; the personnel at D. B. Technology, for its inspiration and encouragement; the faculty and students at the Career and Technical Institute, a division of the Ocean County (N.J.) Vocational-Technical School, for their help in reviewing the book; Tom Seifert, who worked so patiently with me and helped to review the material; Seth Oberman, who created the layout of the book with his desktop publishing talents using Ventura Publisher; John Chiaglia, for his support and encouragement; Dennis Helms, for his legal advice; Theron Shreve, senior editor of computer books at McGraw-Hill, Inc.; Nancy Sileo, associate editor of computer books at McGraw-Hill, Inc; and especially Dora, for her support, love, and computer.

FRANK J. JOHNSON

AutoCAD™ in 3D

INTRODUCTION

This book is designed to help make AutoCAD's powerful 3D features simple and easy to use. It will provide you with the ability to visualize and effectively design in three dimensions using all of AutoCAD's 3D commands.

It will help you to become proficient in drawing on separate planes with AutoCAD's User Coordinate Systems to design and edit 3D wireframe and surface models. You will also learn to shade the models with AutoCAD's rendering program, AutoSHADE.

WHY 3D?

Designing and drawing in three dimensions is beneficial to the overall drawing process. Three-dimensional models can be designed within AutoCAD* to better communicate construction ideas. The views of the model can then be extracted and used in other parts of the drawing or on different drawings.

For example, a part can be drawn as a 3D model and viewed as an isometric or perspective drawing. Then with the use of AutoCAD's 3D commands, you can look at the model from any angle to produce as many views as required. You can look at the top, right side, front, and left side elevations. You no longer have to create separate views.

Previous versions of AutoCAD did not have "true 3D" capabilities, therefore you were limited to drawing in 2D. When drawing a 2D orthographic drawing, three separate views were created. The views did not show depth; as a result it was difficult to visualize what the part would look like. AutoCAD could not put the three separate views together and generate a 3D model nor could you draw a model in three dimensions.

Now, with AutoCAD Release 10, you can design a "true 3D" model of an object and rotate the model to display any view desired. Instead of drawing three separate views, you only have to design one 3D model.

It is a common misconception that when using CAD you draw each view separately and the program will automatically generate the isometric or 3D model. Actually it is just the opposite; the 3D model is created and the views are extracted from the model. The designing of one model rather than several views greatly enhances the overall drawing process.

---

* AutoCAD is a registered trademark of Autodesk, Inc.

PREREQUISITES

To effectively design three dimensional models with AutoCAD you should be comfortable with AutoCAD's basic commands for drawing simple two dimensional objects.

You must also understand the concepts of the X and Y axis used within AutoCAD's drawing area (the X-Y plane).

You should know how to set up the correct paper size with the LIMITS command with reference to the size of the part to be drawn.

You should also know how to use AutoCAD's "absolute" and "relative" point specification modes.

You do not need to be an expert, but you should understand how to use AutoCAD's basic commands.

SOFTWARE AND HARDWARE REQUIREMENTS

Depending on the equipment attached to your PC, AutoCAD can operate in either a dual-screen or single-screen mode. In single-screen mode, one monitor will be used for both graphics and text. In dual-screen mode, one monitor is used for text commands and the other is used for drawing.

Standard Configuration*

IBM Personal Computer, PC XT, PC AT, or PS/2 Model 30, 50, 60, or 80 with at least 640K of memory†

- One double sided floppy disk drive and a hard drive
- Intel 8087, 80287, or 80387 math coprocessor
- Supported graphics card
- DOS operating system, version 2.0 or higher, or other operating system that can run AutoCAD
- Asynch communications adapter (serial port)
- Digitizing tablet or mouse
- Plotter
- Printer/plotter with parallel port (optional)
- Hardware lock (for international version of AutoCAD)
- AutoCAD Release 10 or higher

---

* This is from the AutoCAD "Performance and Installation Guide".

† A 80386 processor is recommended.

3D AND AUTOCAD RELEASE 10

Since all AutoCAD drawings start as 2D drawings, the transition from 2D to 3D will be fairly simple for most users. Most 2D drawings can be converted to 3D with some simple editing techniques.

With AutoCAD Release 10 all drawing entities will now have a Z coordinate along with their X and Y coordinates. The X coordinate is the point on the horizontal axis (length), the Y coordinate is the point on the vertical axis (width), and the **Z coordinate** is a point on a **plane** which is **perpendicular to the X and Y axes.** The **Z axis** is considered the thickness (**height**) of the entity. A representation of the X-Y-Z axis is shown on p. 10.

AutoCAD Release 10 will allow you to increase your productivity with new commands to produce several views including perspectives, elevations, and renderings. You will be able to **create separate planes** in space to simplify drawing and thinking in 3D with AutoCAD's **User Coordinate Systems.** Each separate plane will have its own user defined origin and its own distinct X-Y-Z orientation.

AutoCAD also has a new **display command** called **DVIEW** (dynamic view), which is more powerful then ZOOM and VPOINT. **DVIEW** allows you to **dynamically view** a model from any angle or plane. You can also dynamically enlarge or reduce the size of an object with the DVIEW Zoom option, using the pointing device or the keyboard.

The new **VPORTS** (viewports) command allows you to **split the screen** into as many as four separate viewports or windows for real time creation of 3D models. Each viewport can have a different elevation of the model displayed, with the pictorial view in another. As each viewport is edited, all viewports will be updated automatically. Each of the viewport configurations can be saved and recalled at any time.

These topics are discussed in detail in the following pages with illustrations and step-by-step exercises to help you become proficient at drawing in AutoCAD's third dimension.

USING THIS BOOK

This book is divided into nine chapters. Chapter 1 is a basic overview of simple 3D modeling and its incorporation into AutoCAD. It will help with the transition of drawing in 3D with older versions of AutoCAD to drawing in 3D with Releases 10 and 11.

Chapter 2 will give an overview of AutoCAD's 3D commands and show you how to start drawing a simple 3D wireframe model. You will begin drawing a basic model by setting up the drawing parameters, then drawing the PLAN view on the X-Y plane and finally assigning heights to the entities drawn. AutoCAD's 3D display commands will be used to display the model.

Chapter 3 will discuss in detail all of AutoCAD's 3D display commands including VPOINT, PLAN, HIDE, DVIEW, and VPORTS and give examples of each.

Chapter 4 will explain how to create separate drawing planes and manipulate them with AutoCAD's new User Coordinate System (UCS command).

Chapter 5 will explain how to create 3D surface models. You will learn how to create 3D solid faces, 3D polylines, and surface meshes.

Chapter 6 will include some helpful tips to consider when designing 3D models using AutoCAD's new 3D commands. Contrasts in the way AutoCAD may react with 3D entities are discussed.

Chapter 7 will detail how to produce a shaded rendering of a model with the use of Autodesk's shading program AutoSHADE.

Chapter 8 will assist you with plotting the completed 3D model. Differences between 2D and 3D plotting will be reviewed.

Chapter 9 will include three-dimensional drawing exercises to help you practice your new skills.

GUIDELINES FOR USING THE BOOK

If you are an experienced AutoCAD user and have designed some basic 3D models with previous releases of AutoCAD and understand 3D modeling terminology, you should start with Chap. **2, "Getting Started"**.

If you have never created a 3D model with AutoCAD or are an inexperienced user, you should start at the beginning of Chap. 1. Chapter 1 will introduce you to 3D modeling terminology and concepts. It will show you the old way of designing 3D models with previous releases of AutoCAD and then introduce you to the new way.

Each chapter is designed so that you draw step by step. As you go through the book, you will be asked to draw either by entering a command from the keyboard, from the pull-down windows, from the tablet or from the screen menu (**Fig. 1**). If the command is typed in from the keyboard you must press the [ENTER] key. The book will display the message that is displayed at the command prompt line at the bottom of the screen and then you will be told what to use as a response. The format will be similar to the one shown here:

❖ **Command:**ZOOM
 All/Center/Dynamic/Extents/Left/Prev/
 Window/<Scale(X)>:
 type **A [ENTER]**

The command prompt line message will be displayed line by line on the page and the user instructions will be placed directly below the command prompt line. The **boldface** material that follows the word "type" is what you should enter from at the keyboard, as shown above.

[ENTER] represents the RETURN or ENTER key on the keyboard. You will need to **press [ENTER]** after most entries. Figure 1 illustrates the AutoCAD drawing editor (graphics screen).

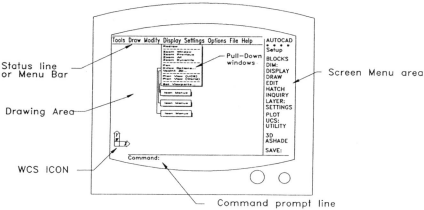

Figure 1 AutoCAD drawing editor.

CHAPTER ONE

OVERVIEW

FROM 2D TO 3D

Three-dimensional drawings on a computer screen can be very deceiving. There are several ways to represent a three-dimensional model.

If you are holding an object in your hand, you can plainly see that it has dimensions to it, such as length, height, and depth. But with a 3D image on a computer screen, the image must be oriented in such a way as to visualize the height, depth, and length of the object. And then, you still may not have a "true three-dimensional" model.

If you look at the object shown below (Fig. 1-1), it appears as if it's set out from the page, but the page is flat. The image is plotted on a flat 2D sheet of paper. So is it really 3D?

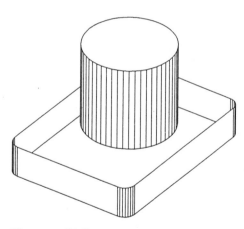

Figure 1-1 3D illusion.

What you have is actually a 2D representation of a 3D image. This drawing is in effect an "optical illusion" to cause your eye to see depth in an image that is actually flat. Your eye can see that this object is a cylinder set on top of a rectangular base. Your mind generates a mental picture of what the drawing wants you to see.

☞ **NOTE:** The general rule is: "WHAT YOU SEE IS NOT ACTUALLY WHAT YOU GET!"

It is simple to draw a quick 3D image with paper and pencil. But to look at this image from other "viewpoints," you would have to draw the image again and again.

With AutoCAD's 3D commands we can change our viewpoint of any drawing image on the screen and look at the object from different angles. We can even simulate a perspective view or create a slide show to create a rotating motion of the object on the screen.

You can now create both 3D drawings and 2D drawings that look like 3D drawings. AutoCAD's 3D commands can be categorized into one of the following:

- Commands to create 3D models
- Commands to view 3D models

3D MODELS

A 3D drawing of an object or a **model** can be created and viewed numerous ways. All **3D models have length, depth, and height (three dimensions).** Although it seems you have designed a very good 3D drawing, you are still restricted to viewing it on a 2D surface, either on the computer screen or on the plotted or printed output. So you only get a representation of the object and not an actual model.

All 3D models on the screen and on paper have lines to describe edges, arcs and circles called **wireframes** as shown below (Fig. 1-2).

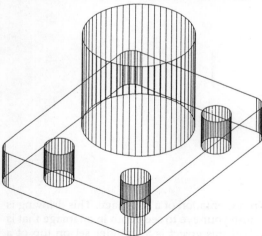

Figure 1-2 3D wireframe model.

These **wireframe models** are basic 3D drawings with "extrusions" to represent simple geometric shapes. Once the wireframe model is constructed, it can be converted to other types of models such as a shaded **surface model** or a **solid model**. Shaded models can be created with the rendering program AutoSHADE and solid models can be created with the solid modeling program AutoSOLID.

Three-dimensional images make it easier to convey construction ideas regardless of how they are created. Recording these images on a computer will help you to produce 3D type views much faster than you could manually on paper.

THE WORLD COORDINATE SYSTEM

Before designing 3D models you must first understand AutoCAD's **World Coordinate System.** The World Coordinate System is defined as the **X-Y plane,** or the cartesian coordinate system, which is used to create all 2D drawings with AutoCAD. It is very similar to working with graph paper with an **X and Y axis.** The X axis is the horizontal direction and the Y axis is the vertical direction. All points are located with an X and Y value in the form (X,Y). The center point, where the X and Y axes intersect is called the origin, indicated by (0,0).

Looking at the AutoCAD drawing editor, the World Coordinate System (WCS) icon is displayed in the **lower left corner** of the screen (Fig. 1-3). It indicates the X and Y axes directions and that the **origin (0,0)** of the drawing is at the lower left corner of the drawing **LIMITS.** As you scroll the pointing device from the lower left corner to the upper right corner of the drawing limits you will see the X and Y values in the coordinate display in the status line change. To toggle the **coordinate display ON** or **OFF** use the **[F6]** function key.

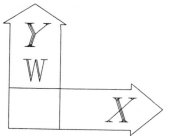

Figure 1-3 World Coordinate System icon.

When creating two-dimensional drawings, all work can be done in this **X-Y plane.** However, if you are working with "true 3D models" a third dimension is required. The Z axis is added to locate 3D points using (X,Y,Z) coordinate triple. The Z axis is perpendicular to the X-Y plane and represents the height, or thickness, of an object.

Below is a representation of the **World Coordinate System** with its new **Z axis** (Fig. 1-4).

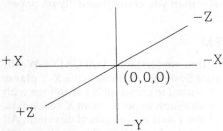

Figure 1-4 X-Y-Z axis.

In addition to the World Coordinate System, AutoCAD Release 10 can have separate User Coordinate Systems which can be defined by the user.

USER COORDINATE SYSTEMS

A User Coordinate System (**UCS**) is similar to the AutoCAD World Coordinate System except the user can define the origin location and the X and Y axes direction. The **UCS** command will be used to define separate coordinate systems within the drawing. The **origin** (0,0) of the user-defined UCS can be located anywhere in the AutoCAD drawing editor. Several of these User Coordinate Systems may be defined and saved.

RIGHT HAND RULE

To better understand this concept AutoCAD uses the **right hand rule** to define all coordinate systems used in a drawing (Fig. 1-5). Place your right hand near the screen with your palm facing you. Extend your thumb in the direction of the positive X axis and point your index finger toward the positive Y axis. Now bend your other fingers down slightly to indicate the positive direction of the Z axis.

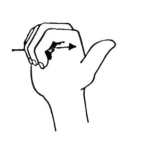 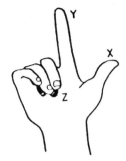

Figure 1-5 Right hand rule.

USING THE NEW Z AXIS

It is best to start all 3D models in AutoCAD's WCS, or the X-Y plane. For example, if you want to draw a simple 3D 1-inch cube, start by drawing a 1-inch square in the original X-Y plane as shown below (Fig. 1-6). This is considered the PLAN view.

Figure 1-6 Cube in PLAN view.

Next, the CHANGE command can be used to change the **thickness**, or height, of the entire square to 1 inch. The result of the CHANGE command will not be obvious from the PLAN view of the World Coordinate System. The square will appear as a cube only when you change your angle of view with the **VPOINT** or **DVIEW** command to allow you to see the added height dimension (Fig. 1-7).

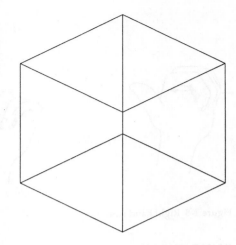

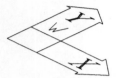

Figure 1-7 3D Cube.

This is a true wireframe representation of a 3D model with length, depth, and height. The height is shown in the **Z axis**, which is always perpendicular to the X-Y plane as shown before. In the PLAN view the positive Z axis is coming out at you from the screen.

TRUE 3D MODELS

A "**true 3D drawing**" or "**model**" is one which can be viewed from any angle or viewpoint to give a true representation of the model. If you were to walk around to the back of the model, you would see what the back side of the model actually looks like. An actual 3D model has three dimensions (length, depth, and height). When building a model, all three of the above dimensions must be considered. The easiest way to design a three-dimensional model with AutoCAD is to draw the top view of the object in PLAN view in the WCS (World Coordinate System) and then assign heights (**thickness**) and **elevations** to its entities as shown in Fig. 1-6 and Fig. 1-7.

The "**elevation**" of an entity in the drawing defines the distance above or below the X-Y plane.

☞   NOTE: The terms **thickness** and **height** are used interchangeably.
             Depth and **width** are also used interchangeably.

VIEWING MODELS

When looking at the models on a screen or paper, you will notice that the image may seem to move (Fig. 1-8). Of course the image does not actually move, but your eyes will play tricks when visualizing a 3D model.

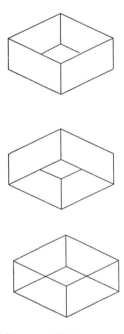

Figure 1-8 3D illusions.

Models can be categorized into three types:

- WIREFRAME
- SURFACE
- SOLID

WIREFRAME MODELS

Wireframe models are basic types of models composed of "**lines**" or "**edges**". The lines used to describe the wireframe models are lines placed in three-dimensional space with the AutoCAD **LINE** command. There are no actual surfaces in the model.

The wireframe model can have an interesting amount of detail and be shown in different colors, rotated, and viewed from different angles. These wireframe models are usually created first, then converted to shaded surface or solid models.

SURFACE MODELS

Surface models are similar to wireframe models except they can have the outside surfaces defined. A surface model is really a wireframe model with boundaries. For example, the surface model below (Fig. 1-9) has its boundaries defined with a wire **mesh**.

Surface models can be used to show colors and shadows as LIGHT sources are directed at them. These types of models are more clearly defined than wireframe models.

Surface models can be created with such AutoCAD commands as the **3DFACE**, **3DMESH**, **TABSURF**, **REVSURF**, and **EDGESURF**. This surface model can then be imported into AutoSHADE and displayed from different angles with the surfaces shaded. AutoSHADE will be discussed in Chap. 7.

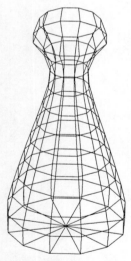

Figure 1-9 Surface model.

SOLID MODELS

Solid models are 3D types of models that look much like shaded surface models but have additional properties. Solid models can have properties such as

weight, volume, mass, and density. Calculations can be done with these models to determine areas and volumes.

The solids modeling process can be done with **AutoSOLID,** which is AutoDESK's **solid** modeling package.

THE OLD WAY

With previous versions of AutoCAD the way to draw 3D models was to use the AutoCAD ISOPLANE command, which simply places you on another "plane" in the drawing. The ISOPLANE command allows only three planes in which to draw and their origins cannot be changed. You can draw on the LEFT, TOP, or FRONT planes by changing the direction of the X and Y axes. This command is not actually needed with AutoCAD Release 10.

The ISOPLANE command can be used to select the current "isometric" plane and corresponding axes.

WORKING WITH AUTOCAD ISOPLANES

The AutoCAD ISOPLANE command feature can be accessed through the pull-down windows under SETTINGS. Select drawing aids from the SETTINGS pull-down window. The following dialogue box appears (Fig. 1-10):

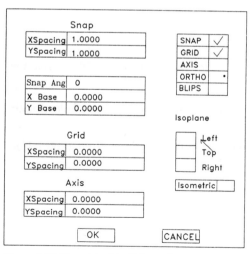

Figure 1-10 Drawing aids dialogue box.

Move the "arrow" into the box next to the word "Isometric" and place a checkmark in the box. Then select OK from the bottom of the dialogue box. Notice the position of the crosshairs and grids.

The three input boxes in this dialogue box refer to three separate planes on which you can draw. The "planes" are **Left, Top, and Front.** If you place a checkmark in the "Top" button box in the dialogue box, the crosshairs will be positioned to let you draw in the TOP view or TOP plane (Horizontal Plane of Projection). The "Left" button box will let you draw in the LEFT view (Profile Plane of Projection). And the "Front" button box will let you draw in the FRONT view (Frontal Plane of Projection).

When drawing in these separate planes, the X and Y axes change to the orientation of the plane you are working in. ORTHO mode is modified to follow the pair of axes corresponding to the current plane.

If you set SNAP style to "isometric", it will set the grid snap to the orientation of the current plane.

☞ NOTE: You may only draw in **one** plane at a time. The ISOPLANE command will not work if the word "Isometric" is not selected from the drawing aids dialogue box.

ISOPLANE COMMAND

The ISOPLANE command can also be activated from the command prompt line. The command format is:

❖ **Command:**ISOPLANE
   left/Top/Right/(Toggle):

☞ NOTE: If you press **[ENTER]**, AutoCAD will toggle you from the current plane to the next. From the LEFT to the TOP, then to the RIGHT plane.

The **[CTRL]** and **[E]**keys used in conjunction with each other will also toggle from the current plane to the next.

The three options are best described by the following illustration (Fig. 1-11):

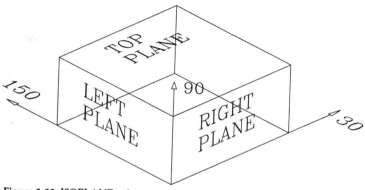

Figure 1-11 ISOPLANE cube.

☞ **NOTE:** It is recommended to use the AutoCAD object snap modes when drawing on different planes.

SUMMARY

The AutoCAD ISOPLANE command is not used throughout the book and should be used only to draw 2D views of 3D objects.

The UCS command is used in place of the ISOPLANE command to control which plane you will work on to create true 3D models.

Chapter 2, **"Getting Started",** will describe how to work with a 3D model with AutoCAD's 3D commands. Many of the AutoCAD 3D commands will be used and then explained in detail in later chapters.

GETTING STARTED

To begin drawing a three-dimensional drawing with AutoCAD you will need to make some mental adjustments as to where to start. The procedure below suggests some AutoCAD settings to draw in 3D.

Follow the steps below to draw a simple 3D model with faces on each side. By rotating the model you'll be able to visualize the effect of the DVIEW and VPOINT commands.

This chapter will show you, step by step, how to draw a three-dimensional model. The commands used will be discussed in detail in later chapters.

SETTING UP TO DRAW IN 3D

Begin a new drawing and name it "MODEL". The following drawing parameters will be used in the procedures outlined below. If you know how to set the drawing UNITS and LIMITS, use the values listed here and proceed to step 5.

UNITS	Decimal
	2 Decimal Places
	Decimal Degrees
	2 Fractional Places For Displaying Angles
	East = 3 O'clock
	Angles Measured Counter Clockwise
LIMITS	Lower Left=0,0
	Upper Right=12,9 (default)

If you are not familiar with AutoCAD and do not know how to start a drawing using the UNITS and LIMITS commands, follow the procedure outlined here. The [ENTER] key can be used to select AutoCAD default values.

1. From the AutoCAD main menu select item **1 (Begin a NEW drawing)**.

2. Name the drawing "**MODEL**".

3. From the command prompt line type the **UNITS** Command:

❖ **Command:**UNITS

The following is displayed:

System of units:	Examples
1. Scientific	1.55E+01
2. Decimal	15.50
3. Engineering	1'-3.50"
4. Architectural	1'-3 1/2"
5. Fractional	15 1/2

Enter choice, 1 to 5 <default>:
type **2 [ENTER]**
Number of digits to right of
decimal point (0 to 8) <default>:
type **2 [ENTER]**

The UNITS command proceeds to angles and displays the following menu:

Systems of angle measure:	Examples
1. Decimal degrees	45.0000
2. Degrees/minutes/seconds	45d0'0"
3. Grads	50.0000g
4. Radians	0.7854r
5. Surveyor's units	N45d0'0" E

Enter choice, 1 to 5 <default>:
type **1 [ENTER]**
Number of fractional places for display of angles (0 to 8)<0>:
type **2 [ENTER]**

After selecting the angle format, the following prompt will appear:

Direction for angle 0.00:

East	3 o'clock	= 0
North	12 o'clock	= 90
West	9 o'clock	= 180
South	6 o'clock	= 270

Enter direction for angle 0 <current>:
press **[ENTER]**

After selecting the angle 0 direction, you'll receive the prompt:

Do you want angles measured clockwise <N>:
press **[ENTER]**

Pressing **[ENTER]** will select the AutoCAD defaults. The defaults indicate that AutoCAD will measure angles in a counterclockwise direction with 0 degrees being due EAST, or at 3 o'clock.

4. Next you should set the **limits**. Enter the LIMITS command:

   ❖ **Command:**LIMITS
   ON/OFF/<lower left corner> <0.00,0.00>.
   press **[ENTER]** for lower left corner
   Upper right corner <12.00,9.00>:
   press **[ENTER]**

5. Enter the ZOOM command.

   ❖ **Command:**ZOOM
   All/Center/Dynamic/Extents/
   Left/Prev/Window/<Scale(X)>:
   type **A [ENTER]**

This allows you to view the entire limits of the drawing.

6. Set the **GRID** size to 1 using the GRID command. Type GRID and   press **[ENTER]**.

   ❖ **Command:** GRID
   Grid spacing(X) or ON/OFF/Snap/Aspect <0.0000>:
   type **1 [ENTER]**

7. Set the **SNAP** to 1 using the SNAP command. Type SNAP and press **[ENTER]**.

   ❖ **Command:** SNAP
   Snap spacing or ON/OFF/Aspect/Rotate/Style <1.0000>:
   type **1 [ENTER]**

DRAWING THE BASIC 3D MODEL

Next, make sure that GRIDS is ON (press **[F7]**) and draw the simple 3D model shown in Fig. 2-1 following this procedure (use ORTHO or SNAP if needed):

1. Enter the **LINE** command and draw a 3-inch square in the center of the screen (Fig. 2-1).

Figure 2-1 Starting a 3D model.

2. Enter the **CIRCLE** command and draw a circle in the center of the square with a radius of .5 (circle does not have to be exactly in the center of the square). Notice the direction of the **WCS** icon at the lower left corner of the screen. The **X** axis is horizontal and the **Y** axis is vertical as usual (Fig. 2-2).

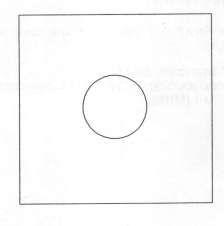

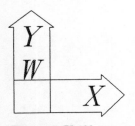

Figure 2-2 PLAN view.

3. Now enter the **CHANGE** command.

  ❖ **Command:**CHANGE
  Select objects:
  pick the square only **[ENTER]**
  Properties/<change point>:
  type **P [ENTER]**
  Change what property(Color/Elev/LAyer /LType/Thickness) ?:
  type **TH for thickness [ENTER]**
  New Thickness <0.0000>:
  type **1.5 [ENTER]**
  press **[ENTER]** to exit CHANGE command.

4. Reenter the **CHANGE** command and change the circle to a **thickness** of 1
   and an **elevation** of 1.5.

  ❖ **Command:**CHANGE
  Select objects:
  pick the circle **[ENTER]**
  Properties/<change point>:
  type **P [ENTER]**
  Change what property(Color/Elev/LAyer /LType/Thickness) ?:
  type **TH for thickness [ENTER]**
  New Thickness<0.0000>:
  type **1 [ENTER]**
  Change what property(Color/Elev/LAyer /LType/Thickness)?:
  type **E for Elevation [ENTER]**
  New Elevation:
  type **1.5 [ENTER]**
  press **[ENTER]** again to exit CHANGE command

5. Enter the VPOINT command from the command prompt line.

  ❖ **Command:**VPOINT
  Rotate/<View point> <0,0,1>:
  type **1,-1,1,** then **[ENTER]**

The object should look like Fig. 2-3 .

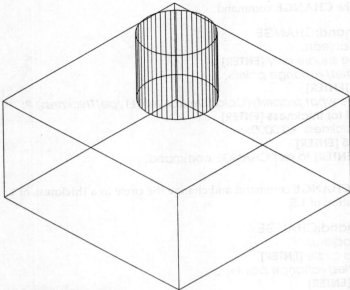

Figure 2-3 3D viewpoint.

The drawing which was drawn in the WCS (X-Y plane) is now a **"true 3D"** wireframe model with a different **thickness** and **elevation** set for both the circle and square.

The **elevation** of the circle is set at 1.5, which causes the circle to appear on the top of the base (square).

Use the **HIDE** command at the command prompt line for hidden line removal. Type **HIDE**.

❖ **Command:**HIDE
Regenerating drawing
Removing hidden lines

The HIDE command performs a hidden line removal on the drawing. Next use the **PLAN** command to restore the original view of the drawing.

❖ **Command:**PLAN
<Current UCS>/UCS/World:
press **[ENTER]**

This returns you to the PLAN or the top, view of the model. Use **ZOOM** with the **A** (all) option to view the entire limits again (Fig. 2-4).

❖ **Command:**ZOOM
All/Center/Dynamic/Extents/Left/Prev/Window/<Scale(X)>:
type **A [ENTER]**

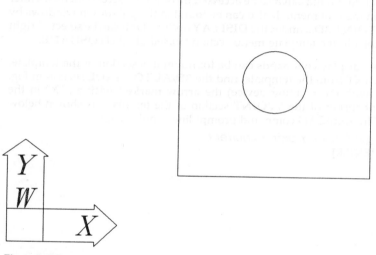

Figure 2-4 Returning to PLAN view.

☞ **NOTE:** The **elevation** and **thickness** can be set by using the **ELEV** (elevation) command before drawing the square and circle to eliminate using the CHANGE command if desired. However, the elevation should be set back to **0** after using it.

LOOKING AT THE 3D MODEL

There are several AutoCAD commands that can be used to view the model:

- VPOINT
- DVIEW
- VPORTS
- PLAN
- HIDE

Some of these commands you are probably very familiar with; however, they will be discussed here briefly and in detail later.

VPOINT COMMAND

The **VPOINT** command was used above and has been with AutoCAD for a while now. In the above example we used the VPOINT command from the command prompt line with a viewpoint of (1,-1,1) for our viewpoint in X,Y,Z values.

The VPOINT command can also be accessed through the screen menus, under **DISPLAY** in the root menu. It also can be found in the pull-down windows by selecting **VPOINT 3D...** under the **DISPLAY** option. Or it can be selected right from the tablet in the template menu section labeled **3D/AUTOSHADE**.

All of the 3D display commands can be found on this section of the template. To use VPOINT from the template, find the **3D/AUTOSHADE** section in Fig. 2-5. Select (with the pointing device) the **arrow marked with an "X"** in the bottom right corner of the **VPOINT** section of the template as shown below (Fig. 2-5). The AutoCAD command prompt line should read:

Enter angle from X-Y plane <current>:
type **30 [ENTER]**

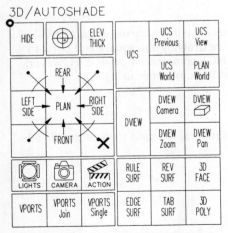

Figure 2-5 3D/AUTOSHADE template section.

To use VPOINT from the pull-down windows select **DISPLAY** from the top of the screen, then select **VPOINT 3D....**

From the dialogue box that appears select the **arrow** pointing from the right to the center (Fig. 2-6). The AutoCAD command prompt line should read:

Enter angle from X-Y plane <current>:
type **30 [ENTER]**

Figure 2-6 3D VPOINT dialogue box selection.

Try all of the **VPOINT** options shown. If you select the lower right "**arrow**" box, here, (Fig. 2-6) and enter a value of 30 degrees for the angle up from the X-Y plane, you will get a "viewpoint" of **(1,-1,1)** as shown before. This will give your best view of a model. Rotate the model back to a viewpoint of (1,-1,1) and continue.

DVIEW COMMAND

The **DVIEW** command (dynamic view) is a more effective way of viewing the model. It offers more choices for viewing a 3D model. To use DVIEW enter the DVIEW command:

❖ **Command:**DVIEW
   Select objects:
   type **C** for crossing and place a **window around object,** then press **[ENTER]**
   Select objects:
   press **[ENTER]**
   Camera/TArget/Distance/POints/PAn Zoom/TWist/CLip/Hide/Off/Undo/<eXit>:
   type **CA [ENTER]**
   Enter angle from X-Y plane<-90.00>:
   type **35 [ENTER]**
   Enter angle in X-Y plane from X axis<-90.00>:
   type **-35 [ENTER]**

The DVIEW command is similar to the VPOINT command but has more options. A **scroll bar** is first displayed on the side and then on the top of the screen to control the "**CAMERA**" angle (Fig. 2-7). You can use the pointing device or type in values at the keyboard.

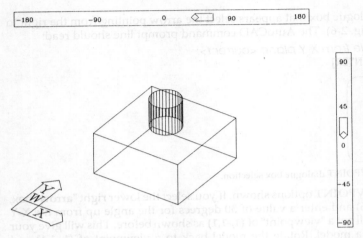

Figure 2-7 DVIEW command scroll bars.

PANNING

The PAN option under DVIEW can be used to move the object around on the screen. Enter the PAN option from the command prompt line.

Camera/TArget/Distance/POints/PAn
/Zoom/TWist/CLip/Hide/Off/Undo/<eXit>:
type **PAn [ENTER]**
Displacement base point:
Second point:

Position the crosshairs in the middle of the "MODEL" and pick to move it downward. The drawing will dynamically move as you move the crosshairs. Select the new location in the center of the screen for the second point and then "pick".

DVIEW ZOOM

The ZOOM option under DVIEW will display a scroll bar similar to the scroll bar displayed under the CAMERA option. You can use the pointing device to increase the "zoom factor" or key in a value at the keyboard. Enter the ZOOM option from the command prompt line.

Camera/TArget/Distance/POints/PAn
/Zoom/TWist/CLip/Hide/Off/Undo/<eXit>:
type **Zoom [ENTER]**
Adjust zoom scale factor <1> :

Use the ZOOM option with the scroll bars by slowly moving the pointing device left and right. Use a ZOOM factor that will display the entire drawing on the screen, then "pick". Now **exit** the DVIEW command by pressing **[ENTER]**.

Camera/TArget/Distance/POints/PAn/PAn/Zoom/TWist/CLip/Hide /Off/Undo/ <eXit>:
press **[ENTER]**

SPLITTING THE SCREEN

Next, we can split the screen into several "sections" called "viewports" to get multiple views at different angles at the same time. This is necessary to enable us to draw on separate planes effectively. To split the screens enter the VPORTS command from the command prompt line.

❖ **Command:**VPORTS
Save/Restore/Delete/Join/Single/?/2/<3>/4:
type **4 [ENTER]**

This will create four separate "**windows**" of the same drawing as shown below (Fig. 2-8). We can work in each of the "viewports" separately.

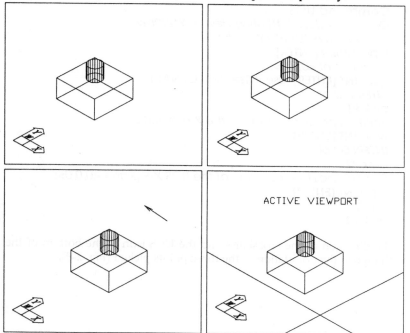

Figure 2-8 Four viewports.

Move the pointing device from one viewport to the next. Notice that the crosshairs will change to an arrow in three of the viewports. Place the pointing device in the viewport where the **crosshairs** appear. This is the **active viewport** and is the only viewport we can work in.

To make another viewport the active one, move the pointing device to the next viewport and "pick". This now becomes the active viewport.

All AutoCAD commands will only effect the active viewport and only one viewport can be active at a time.

USING VIEWPORTS AND UCS

Find the active viewport. It should be the lower right window. If it is not active, make it the active viewport by placing the arrow in the lower right viewport and selecting it with the pick button. You will now work in this viewport.

In order to draw on the separate sides of the model we need to create **separate planes.** We will create a separate plane for each viewport. To do this we will use the **UCS (User Coordinate System)** command.

Enter the UCS command from the command prompt line.

> ❖ **Command:**UCS
>   *Origin/Zaxis/3point/Entity/View/X/Y/Z/Prev/*
>   *Restore/Save/Del/?<World>:*
>   type **3Point [ENTER]**
>   *Origin point <0,0,0>:*
>   type **INT [ENTER]** (use INTsection OSNAP)
>   *INTERSEC of*
>   pick **P1**
>   *Point on positive portion of the X-axis<0,0,0>:*
>   type **INT [ENTER]**
>   ***INTERSEC of***
>   pick **P2**
>   *Point on positive-Y portion of the UCS X-Y plane <0,0,0>:*
>   type **INT [ENTER]**
>   *INTERSEC of*
>   pick **P3**

Notice the direction of the crosshairs and the UCS icon at the bottom of the screen change to the orientation of the three points picked (Fig. 2-9).

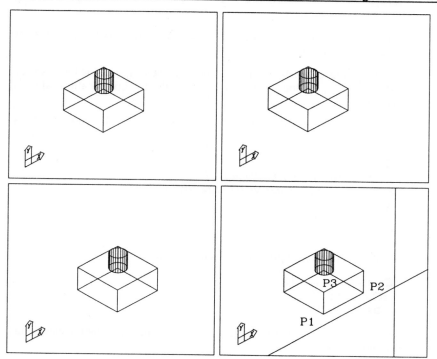

Figure 2-9 Right side UCS.

P1 is the origin of the new UCS. **P2** indicates the positive X direction and **P3** indicates the positive Y direction of the new UCS.

To move the icon to the point **P1 (origin)** selected, enter the **UCSICON** command at the command prompt line.

❖ **Command:**UCSICON
ON/OFF/All/Noorigin/ORigin<current ON/OFF state>:
type **OR [ENTER]**

The **Origin** option will place the **icon** of the new **UCS** at its indicated origin location **P1**.

Now use the UCSICON command again with the **A** (all) option to ensure that all UCS icons in all viewports will appear at their origin locations. Reenter the UCSICON command.

❖ **Command:**UCSICON
ON/OFF/All/Noorigin/ORigin <current ON/OFF state>:
type **A [ENTER]**
ON/OFF/All/Noorigin/ORigin <current ON/OFF state>:
type **OR [ENTER]**

The UCSICON command controls the display of the Coordinate System icons and will be discussed in Chap. 4.

Notice the directions of the X and Y axes and that the origin of the UCS is now at point P1 (Fig. 2-9). All four icons should be at their origin locations shown in each viewport.

The next step is to "**save**" the **UCS** just created. To do this enter the UCS command again.

❖ **Command:**UCS
   Origin/Zaxis/3point/Entity/View/
   X/Y/Z/Prev/Restore/Save/Del/?<World>:
   type **SAVE [ENTER]**
   ?/Name of UCS:
   type **RIGHT [ENTER]**

Use the **PLAN** command to get a **PLAN view** of the new UCS.

❖ **Command:**PLAN
   <Current UCS>/Ucs/World:
   press **[ENTER]**

ZOOM out the PLAN view of the object in this UCS to give a better view (Fig. 2-10). Use the ZOOM command:

❖ **Command:**ZOOM
   All/Center/Dynamic/Extents/Left/Prev/Window/<Scale(X)>:
   type **.7X [ENTER]**

☞ **NOTE:** Make sure to use a decimal point and 7X.

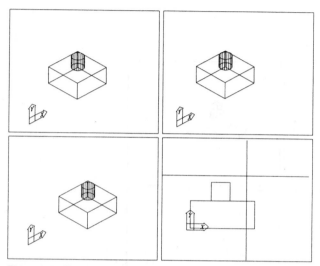

Figure 2-10 Right side PLAN view.

The ZOOM command is used here to place the PLAN view in the center of the viewport.

We have just created "**right side view**" and labeled it **RIGHT**.

Now create a "**front view**" and "**top view**" in the other viewports.

Move the cursor (arrow) to the lower left viewport and pick to make it the active viewport. PAN the model to the center of the viewport if necessary.

Enter the UCS command from the command prompt line again and look at Fig. 2-11.

❖ **Command:**UCS
Origin/Zaxis/3point/Entity/View/X/Y/Z/Prev/
Restore/Save/Del/?<World>:
type **3Point [ENTER]**
Origin point <0,0,0>:
type **INT [ENTER]**
INTERSEC of
pick **P1**
Point on positive portion of X-axis<0,0,0>:

type **INT [ENTER]**
INTERSEC of
pick **P2**
Point on positive-Y portion of the UCS X-Y plane <0,0,0>:
type **INT [ENTER]**
INTERSEC of
pick **P3**

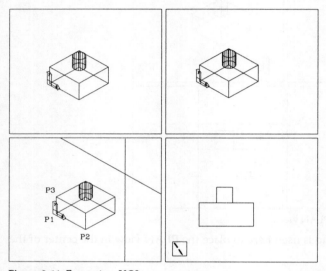

Figure 2-11 Front view UCS.

Notice the direction of the crosshairs and the UCS icon in the lower left viewport change to the orientation of the three points picked. Notice the directions of the X and Y axes and that the **origin** of the UCS is now at point **P1** (Fig. 2-11).

Save the front **UCS** plane just created. To do this enter the UCS command again.

❖ **Command:**UCS
Origin/Zaxis/3point/Entity/View/
X/Y/Z/Prev/Restore/Save/Del/?<World>:
type **Save [ENTER]**
?/Name of UCS:
type **FRONT [ENTER]**

Use the PLAN command to get a plan view of the new UCS.

❖ **Command:**PLAN
   <Current UCS>/Ucs/World:

Press **[ENTER]** to accept the default. Move the PLAN view of the object in this UCS to give a better view (Fig. 2-12). Use the ZOOM command:

❖ **Command:**ZOOM
   All/Center/Dynamic/Extents/
   Left/Prev/Window/<Scale(X)>:
   type **.7X [ENTER]**

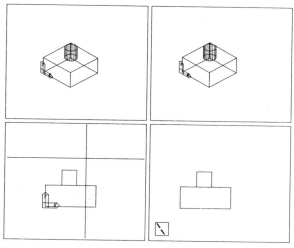

Figure 2-12 Front PLAN view.

Now create the **"top view"**. Move the cursor (arrow) to the upper left viewport and make it the active viewport. PAN the model to the center of the viewport if necessary.

Enter the UCS command from the command prompt line and look at Fig. 2-13.

❖ **Command:**UCS
   Origin/Zaxis/3point/Entity/View/
   X/Y/Z/Prev/Restore/Save/Del/?<World>:
   type **3Point [ENTER]**
   Origin point <0,0,0>:
   type **INT [ENTER]**

INTERSEC of
pick **P1**
Point on positive portion of X-axis<0,0,0>:
type **INT [ENTER]**
INTERSEC of
pick **P2**
Point on positive-Y portion of the UCS X-Y plane<0,0,0>:
type **INT [ENTER]**
INTERSEC of
pick **P3**

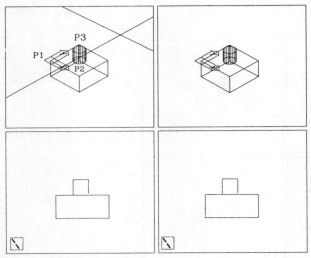

Figure 2-13 Top view UCS.

Notice the direction of the crosshairs and the **UCS icon** change to the orientation of the three points picked. Notice the directions of the X and Y axes and that the **origin** of the UCS is now at point **P1** in the upper left viewport shown above (Fig. 2-13). Save the top UCS plane just created. To do this enter the UCS command again.

❖ **Command:**UCS
Origin/Zaxis/3point/Entity/View/
X/Y/Z/Prev/Restore/Save/Del/?<World>:
type **Save [ENTER]**
?/Name of UCS:
type **TOP [ENTER]**

Use the PLAN command to get a PLAN view of the new UCS.

❖ **Command:**PLAN
   <Current UCS>/Ucs/World:
   press **[ENTER]**

Move the PLAN view of the object in this UCS to give a better view (Fig. 2-14).
Use the ZOOM command:

❖ **Command:**ZOOM
   All/Center/Dynamic/Extents/
   Left/Prev/Window/<Scale(X)>:
   type **.7X [ENTER]**

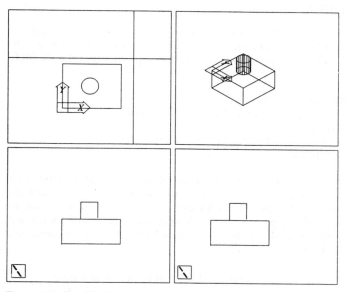

Figure 2-14 Top PLAN view.

Notice that the icons in the other viewports may change to a "box" with a small
"broken pencil" as you change from viewport to viewport and from UCS to
UCS (Fig. 2-14). The **"broken pencil"** ICON indicates that you **cannot draw** in
that particular viewport while working in this current UCS.

☞   NOTE: If you try to draw in these viewports, you may not get the
        desired results.

SAVING THE VIEWPORT CONFIGURATION

We can save the configuration of the current viewports shown in Fig. 2-14 by using the **VPORTS** command.

Enter the VPORTS command:

❖ **Command:**VPORTS
Save/Restore/Delete/Join/Single/?/2/<3>/4:
type **Save [ENTER]**
?/Name for new viewport configuration:
type **VP1 [ENTER]**

Now reenter the VPORTS command and set the screen to a single viewport again.

❖ **Command:**VPORTS
Save/Restore/Delete/Join/Single/?/2/<3>/4:
type **SI [ENTER]**

Notice that the previously active viewport now becomes the whole screen. To look at the **"viewports configuration"** previously saved as **VP1** you will need to reenter the **VPORTS** command with the **"restore"** option. Enter the VPORTS command again.

❖ **Command:**VPORTS
Save/Restore/Delete/Join/Single/?/2/<3>/4:
type **R [ENTER]**
?/Name of viewport configuration to restore:
type **VP1 [ENTER]**

An unlimited number of **"viewports"** can be saved and later restored using the VPORTS command. The VPORTS command can also be activated through the **pull-down** windows under the **DISPLAY** option. Select **DISPLAY** from the pull-down window at the top of the AutoCAD drawing editor and then select **Set Viewports**. From the dialogue box you can select the viewport configuration desired. Select **Exit**.

☞ **NOTE:** Only one viewport and one UCS can be active at a time.

DRAWING ON THE FACES OF THE MODEL

SEPARATING LAYERS

Now we can draw on the separate planes which we just created. First make sure you have restored the **"viewport"** called **"VP1"**.

Now, create the following layers with these color assignments:

Layer Name	Color
Front	Red (1)
Right	Yellow (2)
Top	Green (3)

The best way to create layers is to select the **SETTINGS** option from the pull-down window. Then select **MODIFY LAYER**. The **layer** dialogue box appears (Fig. 2-15).

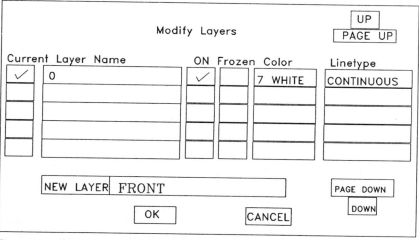

Figure 2-15 MODIFY LAYER dialogue box.

Place the arrow in the **new layer** box at the bottom and type in each of the new layer names, i.e., FRONT [ENTER], TOP [ENTER], RIGHT [ENTER]. Assign the colors shown above to the layer names by placing the arrow in the color box (white) and pressing the pick button. When the color dialogue box appears, place a checkmark in the column to the left of the desired color, then select **OK**. Do this for each layer name.

Now make the layer **FRONT** the **current layer** by placing a checkmark in the box in front of the layer name "FRONT". Select **OK** from the first layer dialogue box to exit and save the new layer names and colors.

WORKING WITH UCS

In order to draw on the faces of the MODEL you will have to change to the UCS or plane you wish to draw on. You can only draw on the separate faces of the MODEL one at a time.

Select **SETTINGS** from the pull-down window. Then select **UCS DIALOGUE**. The following dialogue box appears (Fig. 2-16).

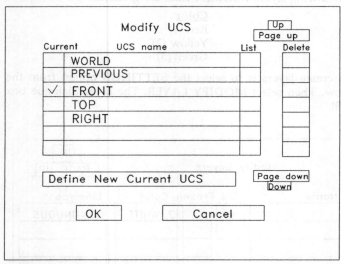

Figure 2-16 UCS dialogue box.

Notice that the names of the User Coordinate Systems we created are listed. To make the UCS called **FRONT** the **current UCS**, place a checkmark in the box to the left of the name FRONT, then select OK at the bottom.

Now make the **lower left "viewport"** the **active** viewport by moving the arrow to the lower left window on the screen and press the pick button. We can now draw in the UCS called FRONT in the active viewport.

Draw a **circle** with a **radius** of **.5** on the base of the object in the **FRONT** view **(lower left viewport)**. Notice the changes in the other viewports. The circle appears as a circle in the front view, a line or edge in the top and right side views, and an ellipse in the 3D model (Fig. 2-17).

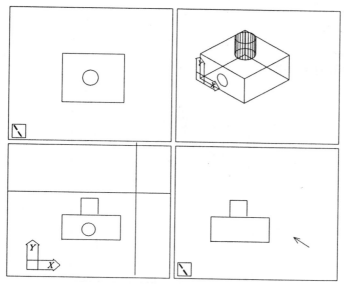

Figure 2-17 Completed 3D model.

Now make the **lower right viewport** the **active** viewport. Change the **current UCS** to **RIGHT** with the UCS dialogue box. Also use the Modify Layer dialogue box to make the **current layer RIGHT**.

☞ **NOTE:** Dialogue boxes are accessed by selecting **Settings** from the pull-down windows.

ADDING THE FACES

Surfaces can be drawn on any UCS using the **3DFACE** command. To draw a face on the right side view, enter the 3DFACE command and look at Fig. 2-18.

❖ **Command:**3DFACE
First point:
type **INT [ENTER]**
INTERSEC of
pick **P1**
Second point:
type **INT [ENTER]**
INTERSEC of
pick **P2**
Third point:
type **INT [ENTER]**
INTERSEC of
pick **P3**
Fourth point:
type **INT [ENTER]**

INTERSEC of
pick **P4**
Third point:
press **[ENTER]** to exit

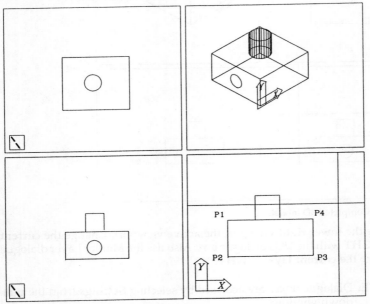

Figure 2-18 3DFACE in right side view.

The **3DFACE** command is similar to the **SOLID** command. It creates a solid
face on an object. The 3DFACE created is a single entity.

We can **HATCH** the 3DFACE we just created. Enter the **HATCH** command.
Select the option DRAW from the pull-down window, then select HATCH...
Select the BRICK pattern.

The following appears at the command prompt line:

Pattern (? or name/U,style) <current>: BRICK
Scale for pattern<1.0000>:
press **[ENTER]**
Angle for pattern :
press **[ENTER]**
Select objects:
pick the 3dface
Select objects:
press **[ENTER]** to exit HATCH

The 3DFACE in the lower right viewport should now be hatched (Fig. 2-19).

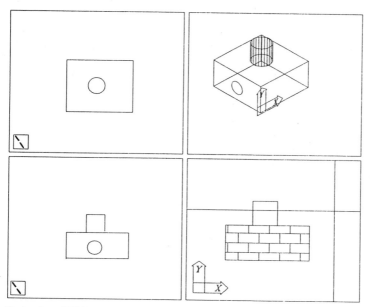

Figure 2-19 BRICK hatch pattern on 3DFACE.

Now make the **upper left viewport** the **active** viewport. Change the **current UCS** to **TOP** with the UCS dialogue box. Also use the Modify Layer dialogue box to make the **current layer TOP**.

Draw a face on the top view in the upper left viewport with the 3DFACE command (Fig. 2-20).

❖ **Command:**3DFACE
   First point:
   type **INT [ENTER]**
   INTERSEC of
   pick **P1**
   Second point:
   type **INT [ENTER]**
   INTERSEC of
   pick **P2**
   Third point:
   type **INT [ENTER]**
   INTERSEC of
   pick **P3**
   Fourth point:
   type **INT [ENTER]**
   INTERSEC of
   pick **P4**
   Third point:
   press **[ENTER]** to exit

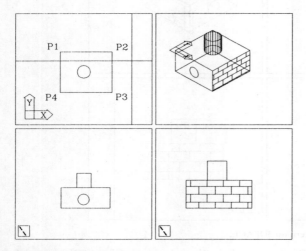

Figure 2-20 3DFACE in top view.

HATCH the 3DFACE you just created using the 3DFACE and the circle as the boundaries to hatch. Enter the **HATCH** command from the pull-down windows. Select the **ANSI37 pattern** (see Fig. 2-21).

The following appears at the command prompt line:

Pattern (? or name/U,style)<current>:
select **ANSI37**
Scale for pattern<1.000>:
press **[ENTER]**
Angle for pattern <1.000>:
press **[ENTER]**
Select objects:
pick the 3dface
Select objects:
pick circle
Select objects:
press **[ENTER]**

The new 3DFACE created in the TOP view is now hatched with the ANSI37 pattern. Notice how all viewports are affected by the changes (Fig. 2-21).

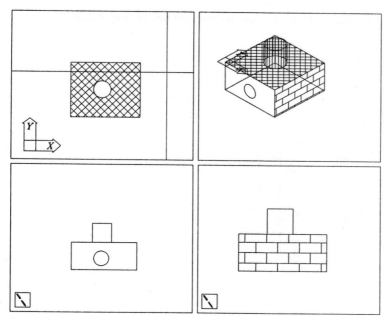

Figure 2-21 3DFACE with ANSI37 hatch pattern.

Now, change the **current viewport** to the **upper right viewport** (where the 3D model is) and use the **HIDE** command to remove all hidden lines. Type HIDE.

❖ **Command:**HIDE
Regenerating drawing
Removing hidden lines

You have now created your first **"true 3D model"**. You can change your viewpoint of the model with the VPOINT or DVIEW commands. But first return to a **SINGLE** viewport. Enter the **VPORTS** command by selecting **DISPLAY** from the pull-down windows, then select **Set Viewports...** Pick the single viewport option from the dialogue box. You will need to use the HIDE command again in a single viewport to remove hidden lines.

The "**MODEL**" drawing should look like the one below (Fig. 2-22):

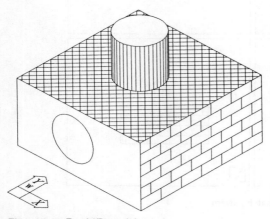

Figure 2-22 Final 3D model.

Now you can use **VPOINT** or **DVIEW** to rotate the model to any desired angle. Before saving the drawing to the disk, use the UCS command to restore the World Coordinate System. Enter the UCS command.

❖ **Command:**UCS
Origin/Zaxis/3point/Entity/View/
X/Y/Z/Prev/Restore/Save/Del/?<World>:
press **[ENTER]**

Save the drawing with the name "**MODEL**".

❖ **Command:**SAVE
File name :
type **MODEL [ENTER]**

☞ **NOTE:** The **END** or **QUIT** command can be used to exit the AutoCAD drawing editor.

SUMMARY

The procedures in this chapter have used only some of the options available with AutoCAD's 3D commands. The options to all of the commands will be explained in the chapters that follow.

Chapter 3 will use and explain all of the AutoCAD **3D display commands** and their options. The VPOINT, DVIEW, PLAN, HIDE, and VPORTS commands will be discussed in greater detail.

These commands can be used to rotate the display of the 3D model or to change your viewpoint.

3D DISPLAY COMMANDS

This chapter will discuss the AutoCAD commands used to change your view of a model during and after it is created. In order to accurately describe a 3D model you must be able to view it from any desired angle. We can do this with the AutoCAD display commands.

First, we can change our "point of view" with the **VPOINT** or (viewpoint) command. We can also select any portion of the object to view at different angles with the **DVIEW** (dynamic view) command.

VIEWING WITH THE VPOINT COMMAND

The **VPOINT** command was used in Chap. 2 and has been with AutoCAD for some time now. The **VPOINT** command is used to change your viewpoint when looking at an object on the screen.

The **VPOINT** command can be accessed from the root screen menu, under **DISPLAY**, from the template under the menu called **3D/AUTOSHADE** or from the **pull-down windows** under the **DISPLAY** option.

Let's try some of the VPOINT command options.

Load the drawing "**MODEL**", which you created in the Chapter 2.

From the AutoCAD main menu, select **2 "Edit an EXISTING drawing"**. Then type **MODEL** for the **NAME** of drawing.

☞ NOTE: The VPORTS, UCS, and VPOINT commands described here may not be needed if the drawing from Chap. 2 was saved with the WCS current in a single viewport as shown in Fig. 3-1.

To make sure the entire drawing is shown on the screen use the VPORTS (viewports) command to display a **single screen** if necessary. Type VPORTS.

❖ **Command:**VPORTS
 Save/Restore/Delete/Join/Single/?/2/<3>/4:
 type **Si [ENTER]**

You should now have a single screen view. Now use the UCS command to ensure you are in the World Coordinate System (WCS). Type the UCS command at the command prompt line.

❖ **Command:**UCS
 Origin/Zaxis/3point/Entity/View/X/Y/Z/Prev/
 Restore/Save/Del/?<World>:
 press **[ENTER]**

This sets the World Coordinate System as current. Now use the **VPOINT** command to change the display of the model by typing **VPOINT** at the command prompt line.

❖ **Command:**VPOINT
   Rotate/<View point><0.00,0.00,0.00>:
   type **1,-1,1 [ENTER]**

This will give you the best view of a 3D model. These values are considered X, Y, and Z values.

Now use the ZOOM command with a scale factor of .7x to reduce the model down a bit.

❖ **Command:**ZOOM
   All/Center/Dynamic/Extents/
   Left/Prev/Window/<Scale(X)>:
   type **.7x [ENTER]**

The display should look something like this (Fig. 3-1):

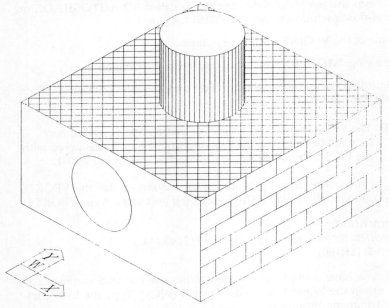

Figure 3-1 3D viewpoint of model.

Notice the direction of the WCS icon and the crosshairs.

ROTATE OPTION

From the root screen menu (side screen menu), select **DISPLAY**, then select **VPOINT**. The **Rotate** option under VPOINT will allow you to rotate the object around a specified point (pivot point). Choose the **rotate** option, and the following prompts will appear. Enter the indicated values.

❖ **Command:**VPOINT
  Rotate/<View point><0.00,0.00,0.00>:
  type **Rotate [ENTER]**
  Enter angle from X-Y plane from X axis <315.00>:
  type **35 [ENTER]**
  Enter angle from X-Y plane <35.26>:
  type **35 [ENTER]**

Notice that the direction of the WCS icon changes from Fig. 3-1.

You can key in any angles desired. The two requested angles are illustrated below (Fig. 3-2).

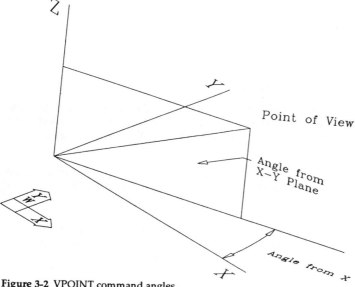

Figure 3-2 VPOINT command angles.

USING VPOINT FROM THE TEMPLATE

The most effective way to use the AutoCAD **VPOINT** command is from the tablet template section labeled **3D/AUTOSHADE** shown below (Fig. 3-3).

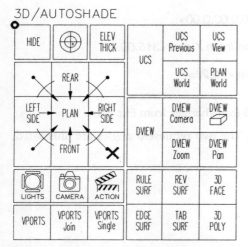

Figure 3-3 3D/AUTOSHADE template section.

Find this section on your tablet. Try the options with the **"arrows"** shown in the template. The arrows point to your viewing direction. As you select each option, you will be prompted to enter the angle from the X-Y plane again. You should enter an angle above **0**.

Select the **arrow** in the box with the **"X"** through it (lower right) and use an angle of **30** for the **"angle from the X-Y plane"**. You will get the same viewpoint as when you typed in (1,-1,1) before.

☞ **NOTE:** If you do not have a tablet, you will have to use the VPOINT option from the screen menu or from the pull-down windows which is explained in the following paragraphs.

USING VPOINT WITH AXES OPTION

To use **VPOINT** from the screen menu select **DISPLAY** from the root screen menu, then **VPOINT** again. The following options appear:

rotate
axes
plan
HIDE:

Select **axes** from the screen menu and the sphere or compass with an axes tripod shown below will appear (Fig. 3-4).

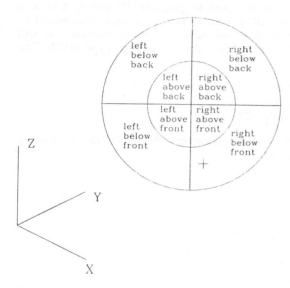

Figure 3-4 VPOINT command sphere and axes.

The center of the "sphere" is called the **north pole** (0,0,1). The inner ring is the **equator** and the outer ring is the **south pole**. You can move the pointing device around to view the object as desired. You will notice that the directions of the X, Y, and Z axes will change as you move the marker. The diagram above shows the views you will get as you position the marker "+" with the pointing device. It will take some time to get used to using this method of **VPOINT** effectively. Select a desired view.

The best way to use the **VPOINT** command is through the **pull-down windows** under the **DISPLAY** option or from the **template** in the section labeled **3D/AUTOSHADE**. They both look and work the same way.

To use **VPOINT** from the pull-down windows, select **DISPLAY** from the menu bar at the top of the screen. Next, select **VPOINT 3D....** The options displayed in the dialogue box are similar and react the same way as the options on the template. Select the icon in the lower right corner with the arrow pointing from the lower right toward the center to produce a view which is the same as typing in (1,-1,1) at the keyboard. After you select the appropriate icon, AutoCAD will prompt:

Enter angle from X-Y plane<0.00>:
type **30 [ENTER]**

HIDE COMMAND

The **HIDE** command is used to **remove "hidden lines"** in a drawing. When the VPOINT or DVIEW commands are used to generate 3D views, it is in a "wireframe" form, meaning that all lines are drawn, even those that would be hidden by other objects. HIDE does not have any subcommands and will regenerate the drawing with the "hidden" lines removed. Type HIDE. The command format is:

❖ **Command:**HIDE
Regenerating drawing.
Removing hidden lines: 125

Try the **HIDE** command now with the drawing called "MODEL" after using the VPOINT command (Fig. 3-5).

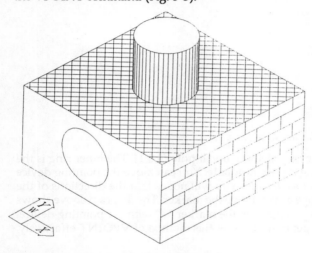

Figure 3-5 Model with hidden lines removed.

PLAN COMMAND

The **PLAN** command is used to return to the **PLAN** view of the drawing (VPOINT 0,0,1). The PLAN view will only change the current UCS to its PLAN view. For example, if you are working in the WCS (World Coordinate System) and you use the PLAN command, it will display the "PLAN", or **TOP**, view of the drawing with respect to the **WCS** only. Remember the WCS is where all AutoCAD drawings are started from. Type **PLAN**.

❖ **Command:**PLAN
<Current UCS>/UCS/World:
press **[ENTER]**

The options are:

Current UCS	<default> This sets the display to the PLAN view of the current User Coordinate System.
UCS	This lets you set the display to the PLAN view of a previously saved UCS.
World	This sets the display to the PLAN view with respect to the World Coordinate System.

☞ **NOTE:** The PLAN command will display the entire drawing extents on the screen.

Use the **ZOOM** command with the **A** (all) option to view the entire drawing limits on the screen. Type ZOOM.

❖ **Command:**ZOOM
All/Center/Dynamic/Extents/
Left/Prev/Window/<Scale(X)>:
type **A [ENTER]**

Using the **PLAN** command with the drawing called "**MODEL**" after using the VPOINT command should give a view which looks like the one below (Fig. 3-6).

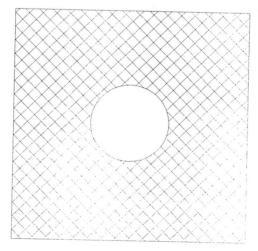

Figure 3-6 PLAN view of model.

Now exit the AutoCAD drawing editor without saving this drawing. Use the **QUIT** command. From the command prompt line type **QUIT**.

❖ **Command:**QUIT
AutoCAD responds with the question:
"Really want to discard all changes to the drawing?"
Type **Y** for yes.

☞ **NOTE:** User Coordinate Systems (UCS command) will be discussed in detail in Chap. 4.

DYNAMIC VIEW

The **DVIEW** command is the most powerful AutoCAD **3D display command** because of its **"dynamic" viewing** capabilities. The DVIEW command can give you a visual perspective view of your drawing dynamically. It allows you to:

- Look at objects with true visual perspective
- Perform hidden line removal with the HIDE command
- "Clip" the display from the front or back of the drawing
- Toggle back and forth between perspective and isometric type views
- PAN and ZOOM within the command
- Specify CAMERA and TARGET points for the CAMERA and adjust a lens length for the CAMERA

DRAWING SETUP

Let's try using the DVIEW command. First set up the following drawing. Start AutoCAD, from the main menu, type **1 "Begin a NEW Drawing"**. Name the drawing **"KITCHEN"**.

Set up the following drawing parameters:

UNITS

ARCHITECTURAL	4
Denominator of smallest fraction:	16
Systems of angle measurement	2 (Degrees/minutes/seconds)
Number of fractional places for display of angles:	2
Direction for angle	0d0': 0d0' (East 3 o'clock)
Angles measure clockwise:	No

LIMITS

Lower left:	0',0'
Upper right:	36',24'

GRID

X spacing =	0'-6"
Y spacing =	0'-6"

SNAP

X spacing =	1'-0"
Y spacing =	1'-0"

Use the following procedure to set up the drawing with the above parameters. The easiest way to set the **GRID** and **SNAP** is to use the **drawing aids** dialogue box under **SETTINGS** in the pull-down windows. From the command prompt line enter the **UNITS** command.

❖ **Command:**UNITS

The following is displayed:

System of units	Examples
1. Scientific	1.55E+01
2. Decimal	15.50
3. Engineering	1'-3.50"
4. Architectural	1'-3 1/2"
5. Fractional	15 1/2

Enter choice, 1 to 5 <default>:
type **4 [ENTER]**
Denominator of smallest fraction to display
(1, 2, 4, 8, 16, 32 or 64)<16>:
press **[ENTER]**

The UNITS command proceeds to angles and displays the following menu:

Systems of angle measure:	Examples
1. Decimal degrees	45.0000
2. Degrees/minutes/seconds	45d0'0"
3. Grads	50.0000g
4. Radians	0.7854r
5. Surveyor's units	N45d0'0" E

Enter choice, 1 to 5 <Default>:
type **2 [ENTER]**
Number of fractional places for
display of angles (0 to 8) <0>:
type **4 [ENTER]**

After selecting the angle format, the following prompt will appear:

Direction for angle <0d0'0">:

East	3 o'clock	= 0
North	12 o'clock	= 90
West	9 o'clock	= 180
South	6 o'clock	= 270

Enter direction for angle <0 d0'0">:
press **[ENTER]**

After selecting the angle 0 direction, you'll receive the prompt:

Do you want angles measured clockwise? <N>:
press **[ENTER]**

Pressing **[ENTER]** will select the AutoCAD defaults. The defaults indicate that AutoCAD will measure angles in a counterclockwise direction with 0 degrees being due EAST or at 3 o'clock.

☞ **NOTE:** Use the **[F1]** key to toggle back to the drawing screen.

Next you should set the **LIMITS**. Enter the LIMITS command:

❖ **Command:**LIMITS
ON/OFF/<lower left corner><0 '-0",0'-0">:
press **[ENTER]** to select the lower left corner
Upper right corner <1'-0",0'-9">:
type **36', 24' [ENTER]**

☞ **NOTE:** Make sure to use the '(foot) mark.

Set the **GRID** size to 6". Type **GRID**.

❖ **Command:**GRID
Grid spacing(X) or ON/OFF/SNAP/Aspect<0'-0">:
type **6" [ENTER]**
Set the SNAP to 6". Type **SNAP**.

❖ **Command:**SNAP
Snap spacing(X) or ON/OFF/Aspect/Rotate/Style <0'-1">:
type **6" [ENTER]**

Make sure the **GRIDS** are **ON [F7]** and use the **ZOOM** command with the **A** (all) option to get the full drawing limits shown on the screen.

Enter the ZOOM command.

❖ **Command:**ZOOM
All/Center/Dynamic/Extents/
Left/Prev/Window/<Scale(X)>:
type **A [ENTER]**

This allows you to view the entire limits of the drawing on the screen.

DRAWING THE FLOOR PLAN

Draw the floor plan in the WCS (World Coordinate System) with the "breaks" for doors approximately as shown (Fig. 3-7). The room size is 20 by 15 feet.

Figure 3-7 Kitchen floor plan (20 by 15 feet).

Use the CHPROP (Change properties) command to assign a **thickness** of 8 feet to the walls of the floorplan. The CHPROP command is used in place of the CHANGE command to set the thickness (property) of an entity. Type CHPROP or select the **Modify** pull-down window at the top of the screen and then scroll down and select **Properties**.

❖ **Command:**CHPROP
Select objects:
type **W** and place a window around all four walls
Select objects:
press **[ENTER]**
Change what property
(Color/Layer\Ltype\Thickness) ?
type **Thickness [ENTER]**
New Thickness<0'-0">:
type **8'[ENTER]**

(Color\Layer\Ltype\Thickness) ?
press **[ENTER]**

☞ **NOTE:** Make sure to use the ' (feet) and " (inch) marks when entering
all height values.

From the pull-down windows select SETTINGS. Then select MODIFY LAYER.
Define a new layer called "Appliances". Assign the color cyan to the layer and
set the layer current. FREEZE layer 0 by placing a checkmark in the box under
the word "Frozen" next to layer 0. Then select OK from the bottom of the
dialogue box. The walls should have disappeared.

Now draw the counter, sink, stove, table, bench, and refrigerator using the
dimensions shown (Fig. 3-8). Place them anywhere you like on the drawing.
You can turn ON the GRIDS **[F7]**, the COORDINATES **[F6]** and SNAP **[F9]** to
help draw the appliances.

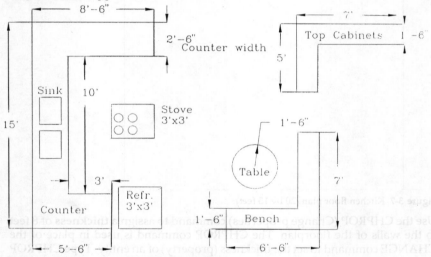

Figure 3-8 Drawing the kitchen appliances.

ASSIGNING HEIGHTS

Do not thaw layer 0 yet. Let's give height dimensions to the appliances. All of
the objects in the floorplan have been drawn in the X-Y plane and have no
height value as of yet.

To give heights enter the **CHANGE** command and assign an **elevation** and
thickness to each of the items as follows. Type CHANGE.

❖ **Command:**CHANGE
   Select objects:

Select the following objects individually, change ELEV and THICKNESS as indicated, then **[ENTER]**

Counter
 ELEV = 0
 THICKNESS = 3′

Refrigerator
 ELEV = 0
 THICKNESS = 6′

Stove   Stove burners (4 circles)
 ELEV = 0   ELEV = 3′
 THICKNESS = 3′   THICKNESS = 0

Table
 ELEV = 0
 THICKNESS = 2′6"

Bench
 ELEV = 0
 THICKNESS = 1′6"

2 Sinks
 ELEV = 3′
 THICKNESS = 0

Cabinets (upper)
 ELEV = 5′
 THICKNESS = 2′

After changing the heights and elevations of all the entities, select SETTINGS from the pull-down windows, then select MODIFY LAYER. **Thaw** layer 0 and place the appliances in the floorplan with the move command as shown (Fig. 3-8). Save the drawing at this point with the SAVE command. Type SAVE at the command prompt line.

❖ **Command:**SAVE
 File name <kitchen>:
 type **KITCHEN [ENTER]**

☞ **NOTE:** Use the OSNAPS command to accurately place each appliance with the MOVE command.

Use the **VPOINT** command to get a parallel isometric view of the kitchen (Fig. 3-9). Type VPOINT.

❖ **Command:**VPOINT
 Rotate/<View point><0′-0",0′-0",0′-1">:
 type **1,-1,1 [ENTER]**

Make sure all heights and thicknesses are correct. If they are not, use the CHANGE command to correct them. The CHANGE command can be used right from this view. The drawing should look like the one below. Use the HIDE command to remove hidden lines. Type HIDE.

❖ **Command:**HIDE
Regenerating drawing.
Removing hidden lines: 75

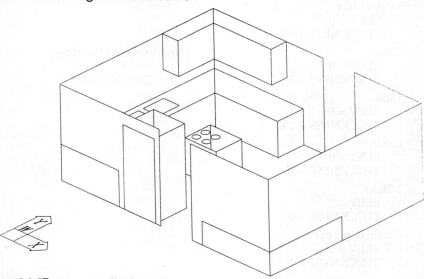

Figure 3-9 3D viewpoint of kitchen.

Once the drawing looks like Fig. 3-9, enter the PLAN command to set the display back to the PLAN view (Fig. 3-10) of the WCS (World Coordinate System). Type PLAN.

❖ **Command:**PLAN
<Current UCS>/UCS/World:
press **[ENTER]**

The current UCS is the WCS or world. Now enter the **ZOOM** command with the **A** (all) option to set the display back to its original size.

❖ **Command:**ZOOM
All/Center/Dynamic/Extents/
Left/Prev/Window/<Scale(X)>:
type **A [ENTER]**

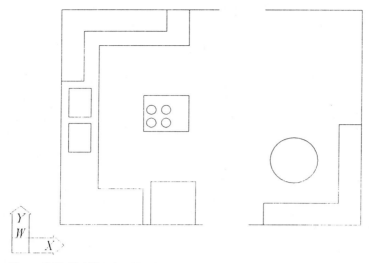

Figure 3-10 PLAN view of kitchen.

The drawing should be "**saved**" again at this point with the **SAVE** command. Type SAVE.

❖ **Command:**SAVE
File name <kitchen>:
type **KITCHEN [ENTER]**

USING THE DVIEW COMMAND

Let's use the **DVIEW** command to change our viewpoint of the kitchen instead of the VPOINT command. Enter the **DVIEW** command from the command prompt line as follows. Type DVIEW.

❖ **Command:**DVIEW
Select objects:
press **[ENTER]**

If you simply press **[ENTER]** here instead of selecting any objects, AutoCAD will **select its own object** called "DVIEWBLOCK" (Fig. 3-11). To let you continue with the command, the AutoCAD selected object is a picture of a house. Whatever rotation, distance, zoom factor, etc., is performed on the house, the same exact settings will be made to your drawing when you exit the **DVIEW** command.

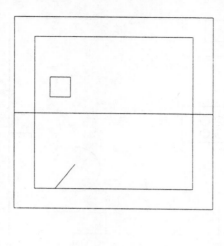

Figure 3-11 AutoCAD DVIEWBLOCK house.

At the command prompt line you are given **12** options.

Camera/TArget/Distance/POints/PAn
/Zoom/TWist/CLip/Hide/Off/Undo/<eXit>:
type **CAmera**
Enter angle from X-Y plane<90.00>:
type **35**
Enter angle in X-Y plane from X axis<-90.00>:
type **35**

The DVIEW command is similar to the VPOINT command but has more options. A **scroll bar** is displayed on the side of the screen first and then on the top to control the **"CAMERA" angle**. You can use the pointing device or type in values at the keyboard. For now, we will type in the values (**35**) used here. Notice that you are still in the DVIEW command. The DVIEWBLOCK house should be orientated like Fig. 3-12 .

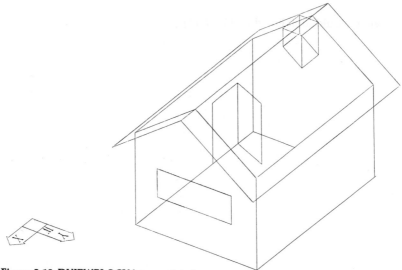

Figure 3-12 DVIEWBLOCK house rotated.

☞ NOTE: Make sure **SNAP** is **OFF** when using the DVIEW command
with the scroll bars or you will not have total control when rotating the object.

Exit the DVIEW command by pressing **[ENTER]**. This will select the default
DVIEW command option (**eXit**).

Use the HIDE command for hidden line removal. Type **HIDE**.

❖ **Command:**HIDE
Regenerating drawing
Removing hidden lines

The drawing should look like this (Fig. 3-13):

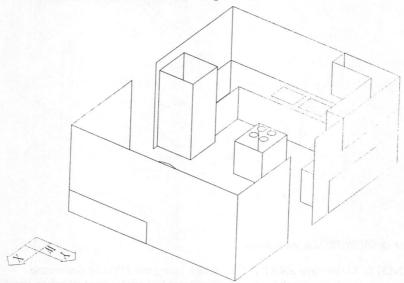

Figure 3-13 Kitchen viewed using the DVIEW command.

☞ **NOTE:** Notice the direction of the UCS icon in the lower left corner of the screen.

POSITIONING THE DRAWING (PAN)

The **PAN** option under **DVIEW** can be used to move the object around on the screen. Reenter the DVIEW command and use the **PAn** option as follows. Type DVIEW and select objects with a crossing window.

❖ **Command:**DVIEW
Select objects:
type **C** for crossing and place a window around the entire drawing.
Select objects:
press **[ENTER]**
*Camera/TArget/Distance/POints/PAn
/Zoom/TWIst/CLip/Hide/Off/Undo/<eXit>:*
type **PAN [ENTER]**
Displacement base point:
pick near the center of kitchen.
Second point:
drag the drawing down slightly on the screen and pick.

When panning with the DVIEW command, position the crosshairs in the middle of the drawing and pick to move it downward. The drawing will **dynamically move** as you move the crosshairs. Pick the new location in the lower center of the screen. Notice you are still in the DVIEW command.

MOVING IN FOR A CLOSER LOOK (ZOOM)

The **ZOOM** option under **DVIEW** will display a **scroll bar** similar to the scroll bar displayed under the CAMERA option. You can move the pointing device to the right to increase the **"zoom factor"** or key in a value at the keyboard. Type **Zoom** from within the DVIEW command.

*Camera/TArget/Distance/POints/PAn
/Zoom/TWist/CLip/Hide/Off/Undo/<eXit>:*
type **Zoom [ENTER]**
Adjust zoom scale factor <1>:
type **2x [ENTER]**

The drawing should look like this (Fig. 3-14).

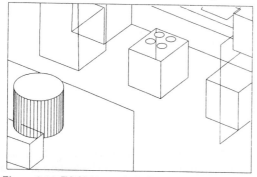

Figure 3-14 ZOOM in with the DVIEW command.

You can also use the **ZOOM** option to **"shrink"** the drawing. To do so, use negative values or move the pointing device to the left of the **1x** in the scroll bar at the top of the screen.

Try the ZOOM option under DVIEW with different values and then try it with the scroll bar by moving left and right with the pointing device. Bring the drawing back to a size that displays the entire room (Fig. 3-15).

Now exit the DVIEW command with the **"eXit"** option under DVIEW. Remember that **eXit** is the default for the DVIEW command. The HIDE command can be used to perform hidden line removal at any time within the DVIEW command.

*Camera/TArget/Distance/POints/PAn
/Zoom/TWist/CLip/Hide/Off/Undo/<eXit>:*
type **X [ENTER]**

Save the "view" with the AutoCAD **VIEW** command. Type VIEW.

❖ **Command:**VIEW
?/Delete/Restore/Save/Window:
type **Save [ENTER]**
View name to save:
type **view1 [ENTER]**

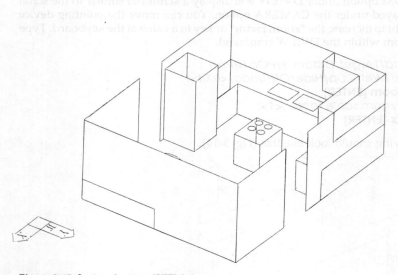

Figure 3-15 Saving the view "VIEW1".

☞ NOTE: When using the DVIEW command, the entire drawing does not
have to be selected. You can use the AutoCAD "selection sets" to
select portions of the drawing to display with the DVIEW
command.

ACCESSING DVIEW

The **DVIEW** command can also be found under the **DISPLAY** option in the
pull-down windows, under **DISPLAY** in the root **screen menu**, and on the
template in the **3D/AUTOSHADE** section.

Select **DISPLAY** from the menu bar at the top of the screen.

Next select **DVIEW Options....**

From the DVIEW dialogue box, select **DVIEW Camera**. AutoCAD prompts:

Select objects:

type **C** for crossing and place a window around the entire drawing,
then press **[ENTER]**.

Move the crosshairs over to the right of the screen or until you can move the small circle up or down in the vertical scroll bar that shows values from **-90 to 90.** As you slowly move the pointing device up and down, you will notice the drawing rotating up and down in front of you. Place the small circle in the scroll bar at **0.** Now you are looking straight at the kitchen floorplan (FRONT ELEVATION). Now move the pointing device up in the scroll bar and place it at about **45** and **"pick".**

Now a scroll bar appears at the top of the screen. Move the circle in the scroll bar left, then right. Notice the orientation of the drawing as you move it from **-180 to 0 to 180** degrees. Place the circle at about **45 degrees** (halfway between 0 and +90) and **"pick".**

Only DVIEW CAMERA, DVIEW ZOOM, and DVIEW PAN are available from the pull-down windows and are three DVIEW subcommands. Notice that not all of the subcommands are available though the pull-down windows.

Reenter the DVIEW command to remove the hidden lines. Type DVIEW.

❖ **Command:**DVIEW
Select objects:
type **C** for crossing and place a window around the entire drawing.
Select objects:
press **[ENTER]**
*Camera/TArget/Distance/POints/PAn
/Zoom/TWist/CLip/Hide/Off/Undo/<eXit>:*
type **HIDE [ENTER]**

This should produce an image of the drawing as shown in Fig. 3-16 . Notice the orientation of the **WCS icon** at the lower left corner of the screen. Whenever there is a "W" shown in the icon, it indicates that you are currently working in the WCS (World Coordinate System).

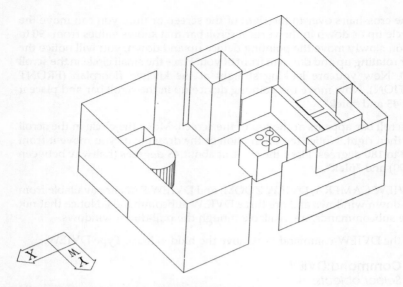

Figure 3-16 Changing the CAMERA angle with DVIEW.

Next, try the **DVIEW options** from the **3D/AUTOSHADE** section of the **template** (if you have one) by selecting them with the pointing device. Use the options **DVIEW CAMERA, DVIEW ZOOM,** and **DVIEW PAN.** They work the same way as shown previously.

Exit the DVIEW command by pressing **[ENTER]**, or type **X,** and then **[ENTER]**.

Camera/TArget/Distance/POints/PAn
/Zoom/TWist/CLip/Hide/Off/Undo/<eXIt>:
type **X [ENTER]**

You should see the "kitchen drawing" on the screen in the orientation that the AutoCAD house was set at (Fig. 3-17).

DVIEW HOUSE

Select the **DVIEW** option with the **icon** of the **"perspective box"** from the template. It is the same as pressing **[ENTER]** immediately after entering DVIEW from the command prompt line, where the AutoCAD (DVIEWBLOCK) **"house"** drawing is used to orientate the display. The **"house"** drawing is shown on the following page (Fig. 3-17) in PLAN view and in perspective.

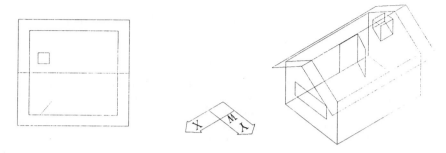

PLAN VIEW

PERSPECTIVE VIEW

Figure 3-17 Plan and perspective view of DVIEWBLOCK house.

Notice that the DVIEW command options appear at the command prompt line. After rotating the house to the desired position and exiting the DVIEW command, the kitchen should reappear positioned on the screen the same way the house was.

Exit the DVIEW command.

Camera/TArget/Distance/POints/PAn
/Zoom/TWlst/CLip/Hide/Off/Undo/<eXit>:
type **X [ENTER]**

You should see the "kitchen drawing" on the screen in the orientation that the AutoCAD house was set at (Fig. 3-17).

SELECTING DVIEW FROM THE SCREEN MENU

To use **DVIEW** from the **screen menu** select **DISPLAY** from the root screen menu, then select **DVIEW**. The following screen menu appears:

DVIEW:

Window
Last
Previous   *(these are the AutoCAD selection sets)*
Crossing
Remove
Add

By Layer

Dviewblk

Dview
Options

If you select the "**By Layer**" option, you will get the following prompt:

Layer name:<Appliances>

Press **[ENTER]** or type a layer name to select objects from.

This option can only be used to select objects to view on a particular layer. The layers must of course be defined first. If you select the "**Dviewblk**" option from the screen menu, the AutoCAD "**house**" drawing appears on the screen, for orientating the display. The house can be orientated with the scroll bars after selecting the **CAmera** option in DVIEW as described before.

If you select "**Dview Options**", the following screen menu appears (you must use the AutoCAD selection sets to select the objects to rotate first and then select "**DVIEW Options**"):

AUTOCAD
* * * *
CAmera
TArget
Distance
POints
PAn
Zoom
TWist
CLip
Hide
Off
Undo
eXit

These are the **12** DVIEW choices as shown previously. Select **eXit**.

You have now used the options **CAMERA, PAN, ZOOM, HIDE,** and **EXIT**. The following section will describe more advanced viewing techniques using the DVIEW command.

POSITIONING THE CAMERA

The following section will explain the remaining **DVIEW** subcommands, which allow you to change your viewpoint of the drawing.

The CAMERA option was used to change your viewpoint of the object. The "object" is considered to be stationary. The CAMERA moves in a vertical direction above or below the object and then left to right. In the previous example your vertical inclination was about **45 degrees**.

Let's look at the kitchen floorplan from another angle. **Restore** the view called "**view1**" with the **VIEW** command. Type VIEW.

❖ **Command:**VIEW
  ?/Delete/Restore/Save/Window:
  type **Restore [ENTER]**
  View name to restore:
  type **view1 [ENTER]**

Now enter the **DVIEW** command. Type DVIEW and enter the information as shown.

❖ **Command:**DVIEW
  Select objects:
  type **C** for crossing, place a window around the entire kitchen, press **[ENTER].**
  Camera/TArget/Distance/POints/PAn
  Zoom/TWist/CLip/Hide/Off/Undo/<eXit>:
  type **CAmera [ENTER]**
  Enter angle from X-Y plane <35.00>:
  type **-35**
  Enter angle in X-Y plane from X axis <35.00>:
  type **35**

  Now type **HIDE** to remove the hidden lines.
  Camera/TArget/Distance/POints/PAn
  /Zoom/TWist/CLip/Hide/Off/Undo/<eXit>:
  type **HIDE [ENTER]**
  The drawing should look like Fig. 3-18.

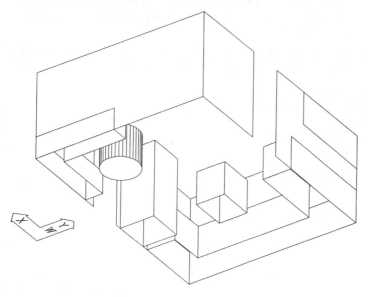

Figure 3-18 Viewing the kitchen from underneath.

It is difficult to see what is really happening with the drawing. Once you remove the hidden lines with the **HIDE** command, it becomes obvious that you are looking at the drawing from underneath. By using the CAMERA option (changing the inclination of the CAMERA by moving the pointing device in the scroll bars) you are keeping the object still and viewing the object from above or below.

Now **eXit** the DVIEW command.

> *Camera/TArget/Distance/POints/PAn*
> */Zoom/TWist/CLip/Hide/Off/Undo/<eXit>:*
> type **X [ENTER]**

It becomes difficult to tell which way is up. The **UCS icon** on the screen will define your angle of view. If the **"arrows"** in the icon crisscross, you are looking from the top. If they don't crisscross, you are looking from underneath. Compare the UCS icons in Fig. 3-16 and Fig. 3-18.

LOOKING AT THE DRAWING IN PERSPECTIVE

The **DVIEW** command also has an option which will produce a true **perspective** view of a drawing. The CAMERA option changed the angle of inclination of the CAMERA to view the object from different viewpoints, from the top down or from the bottom up. However, you may notice that the perspective is not correct.

Viewing a real room from above at a distance would give the appearance that the foreground is slightly larger than the background, as in a perspective view of the object. You can set the AutoCAD display to **"perspective"** mode through the **DISTANCE** option in **DVIEW**.

Let's look at the kitchen in perspective view. First **restore** the previously saved view called **"view1"** with the **VIEW** command. Type VIEW.

> ❖ **Command:**VIEW
> *?/Delete/Restore/Save/Window:*
> type **Restore**
> *View name to restore:*
> type **view1**

The drawing should look like Fig. 3-19 .

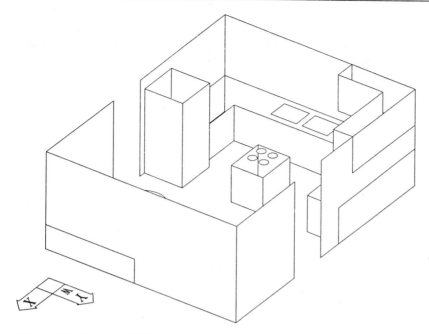

Figure 3-19 Restoring "VIEW1".

Enter the DVIEW command. Type DVIEW.

❖ **Command:**DVIEW
Select objects:
type **C** for crossing, place a window around the entire kitchen
and press **[ENTER]**.
*Camera/TArget/Distance/POints/PAn/
Zoom/TWist/CLip/Hide/Off/Undo/<eXit>:*
type **Distance [ENTER]**

AutoCAD prompts:

New camera/target distance <0'-1">:
type **50' [ENTER]**
Enter the HIDE command.
*Camera/TArget/Distance/POints/PAn/
Zoom/TWist/CLip/Hide/Off/Undo/<eXit>:*
type **HIDE [ENTER]**

Exit the DVIEW command.

*Camera/TArget/Distance/POints/PAn/
Zoom/TWist/CLip/Hide/Off/Undo/<eXit>:*
press **[ENTER]**

The kitchen should look like Fig. 3-20. Notice the difference in the drawing from before using perspective. **The "Distance" option turns perspective ON and sets the distance the camera is from the object.**

The distance set here is 50 feet.

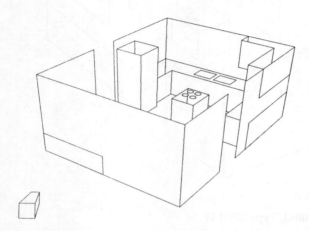

Figure 3-20 Perspective view of the kitchen.

Notice the UCS icon no longer appears on the screen. An oblong box has replaced it. This is to indicate that **perspective** mode is **ON. You cannot draw or edit** the drawing while perspective mode is ON. Pointing and ZOOMing are not allowed when perspective mode is ON. The **Distance** option is used only for viewing purposes.

You can use the VIEW command to save this perspective view of the kitchen. Type VIEW.

❖ **Command:**VIEW
?/Delete/Restore/Save/Window:
type **Save [ENTER]**
View name to save:
type **view2 [ENTER]**

If you go back to the original PLAN view of the drawing to make any edits and, then restore the perspective view (view2), the view will reflect the changes made.

ZOOM WITH PERSPECTIVE

The **ZOOM** option under **DVIEW** will also work in perspective mode.

Use the VIEW command again to restore "**view2**" (this ensures that **view2** is currently displayed on the screen). Type VIEW.

❖ **Command:**VIEW
?/Delete/Restore/Save/Window:
type **Restore [ENTER]**
View name to restore:
type **view2 [ENTER]**

Enter the DVIEW command and use the ZOOM option. Type DVIEW.

❖ **Command:**DVIEW
Select objects:
type **C** for crossing, place a window around the entire kitchen, and press **[ENTER]**.
*Camera/TArget/Distance/POints/PAn
/Zoom/TWist/CLip/Hide/Off/Undo/<eXit>:*
type **ZOOM [ENTER]**
Adjust lenslength <35.00>:
type **150 [ENTER]**

The number you type increases or decreases the zoom factor as if you were looking through a cameras zoom lens. For example, if you entered 150, this would simulate what would happen if you were looking through a 35-mm camera with a 150-mm zoom lens attached.

Type **HIDE** for hidden line removal.

*Camera/TArget/Distance/POints/PAn/
Zoom/TWist/CLip/Hide/Off/Undo/<eXit>:*
type **HIDE [ENTER]**

On the following page is an example of what might be seen looking through a 150-mm zoom lens with hidden lines removed (Fig. 3-21).

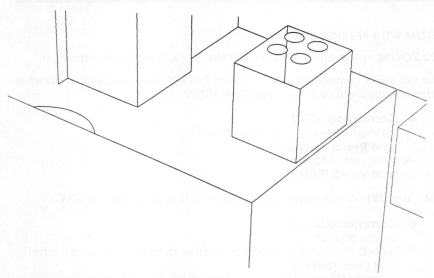

Figure 3-21 ZOOM in perspective mode.

You can also adjust the ZOOM scale factor by moving the pointing device left to right in the scroll bar at the top of the screen. The orientation of drawing remains the same, but the zoom factor changes.

Enter the ZOOM option within the DVIEW command again and move the circle in the scroll bar at the top of the screen to the left to reduce the kitchen so the whole kitchen is displayed on the screen. The zoom factor can also be increased or decreased by typing in zoom factor values at the command prompt line such as **1x, 2x, 6x**, etc.

☞ **NOTE:** It is easiest to use the scroll bars when **zooming** so you can dynamically see the exact level of zoom.

Now **eXit** the DVIEW command.

Camera/TArget/Distance/POints/PAn/
Zoom/TWist/CLip/Hide/Off/Undo/<eXit>:
press **[ENTER]**

Notice that you are still in **perspective** mode.

TARGET OPTION

AutoCAD regards the selected objects as the **"TARGET"**. There is a focal point on the TARGET, typically the center. This TARGET point has an X,Y,Z value in the WCS. You already know how to move the CAMERA. The TARGET option works the same way as CAMERA except that the CAMERA is now stationary and the TARGET moves.

The **TARGET** option is the **opposite** of using the **CAMERA** option. For example, if you move the CAMERA to a position of 35 degrees above the object with CAMERA option, you would be looking down at the object.

If you use TARGET and give a positive 35 degree inclination, then the TARGET is moved 35 degrees above the CAMERA and you are now looking at the object from underneath. Negative TARGET values can be used to simulate positive CAMERA values and vice versa.

USING THE POINTS OPTION

The **POINTS** option within DVIEW can be used to position both the CAMERA and the TARGET. **Perspective** can be **ON** or **OFF**.

Let's use one of the same views as before and try the POINTS option. Restore the view "**view1**" with the VIEW command. Type VIEW.

This will turn **perspective** mode **OFF**.

❖ **Command:**VIEW
   ?/Delete/Restore/Save/Window:
   type **Restore [ENTER]**
   View name to restore:
   type **view1 [ENTER]**

From inside the DVIEW command enter the POINTS option. Type DVIEW.

❖ **Command:**DVIEW
   Select objects:
   type **c** for crossing and place a window around the entire kitchen and press **[ENTER]**.
   Camera/TArget/Distance/POints/PAn/
   Zoom/TWist/CLip/Hide/Off/Undo/<eXit>:
   type **POINTS [ENTER]**
   Enter target point<1.0,1.0,1.0>:
   pick **P1**

AutoCAD will ask for a **TARGET** point. Pick near point **P1** as shown in Fig. 3-22.

AutoCAD prompts:

   Enter camera point<1.0,1.0,1.0>:
   type **.xy [ENTER]**
   of
   pick **P2**
   (need Z):
   type **6' [ENTER]**

Use the AutoCAD filters to pick a CAMERA point location 6 feet above the X-Y plane at P2 as shown above. Enter the **HIDE** command to remove hidden lines (Fig. 3-22). Type **HIDE**.

Camera/TArget/Distance/POints/PAn
/Zoom/TWist/CLip/Hide/Off/Undo/<eXit>:
type **HIDE [ENTER]**

The drawing now looks like the one below (Fig. 3-22).

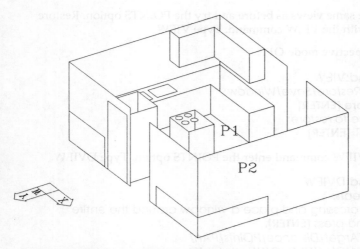

Figure 3-22 Picking CAMERA and TARGET points.

Exit the DVIEW command by pressing **[ENTER]**.

Camera/TArget/Distance/POints/PAn
/Zoom/TWist/CLip/Hide/Off/Undo/<eXit>:
press **[ENTER]**

Save this view with the **VIEW** command as "view3" to use later. Type VIEW.

❖ **Command:**VIEW
   ?/Delete/Restore/Save/Window:
   type **Save [ENTER]**
   View name to save:
   type **view3 [ENTER]**

Restore the view "view1" with the **VIEW** command. Type **VIEW**.

❖ **Command:**VIEW
  ?/Delete/Restore/Save/Window:
  type **Restore [ENTER]**
  View name to restore:
  type **view1 [ENTER]**

Then turn **"perspective mode" ON** with the DISTANCE option in DVIEW. Type DVIEW.

❖ **Command:**DVIEW
  Select objects:
  type **C** for crossing, place a window around the entire kitchen, and press **[ENTER]**.
  *Camera/TArget/Distance/POints/PAn
  /Zoom/TWist/CLip/Hide/Off/Undo/<exit>:*
  type **DISTANCE [ENTER]**
  New camera/target distance <1'-0>:
  type **50'[ENTER]**

Now you have the same view as Fig. 3-20 with "perspective mode" ON. Now enter the **POINTS** option from within the DVIEW command and use points **P1** and **P2** from Fig. 3-22. Type **POINTS.**

  *Camera/TArget/Distance/POints/PAn
  /Zoom/TWist/CLip/Hide/Off/Undo/<eXit>:*
  type **POINTS [ENTER]**
  Enter Target point<0,0,0>:
  pick **P1 [ENTER]**
  Enter camera point<0,0,0>:
  type **.xy [ENTER]**
  of
  pick **P2**
  (need Z)
  type **6'**

Pick points at about the same as points as **P1** and **P2** in Fig. 3-22.

☞ **NOTE:** CAMERA and TARGET points may not be coincident.

Use the ZOOM option in DVIEW to zoom out until you get the desired view (Fig. 3-23). Type ZOOM.

  *Camera/TArget/Distance/POints/PAn/
  Zoom/TWist/CLip/Hide/Off/Undo/<eXit>:*
  type **Zoom [ENTER]**

Move the pointing device to the left of the **1X** in the scroll bar (halfway between 0X and 1X) and "**pick**". Then use the HIDE command to remove the hidden lines (Fig. 3-23).

Camera/TArget/Distance/POints/PAn/
Zoom/TWist/CLip/Hide/Off/Undo/<eXit>:
type **HIDE [ENTER]**

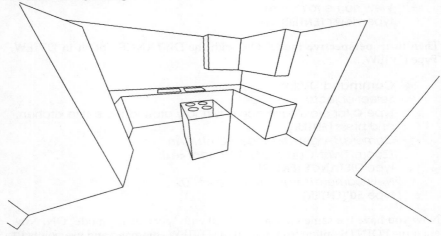

Figure 3-23 Changing the ZOOM level in perspective.

Notice that with **"perspective mode"** turned **ON** (Fig. 3-22), you are almost placed **inside** the kitchen floorplan and with "perspective mode" OFF (Fig. 3-20) you get a slightly different viewpoint, where you are outside looking in. **Exit** the DVIEW command by pressing [ENTER].

Camera/TArget/Distance/POints/PAn/
Zoom/TWist/CLip/Hide/Off/Undo/<eXit>:
press **[ENTER]**

TWIST

The TWIST option will allow you to rotate the drawing left or right around a pivot point (center point) of the drawing or object.

First **restore** the view called **"view1"** with the **VIEW** command again. Type VIEW.

❖ **Command:** VIEW
   ?/Delete/Restore/Save/Window:
   type **Restore [ENTER]**
   View name to restore:
   type **view1 [ENTER]**

Then enter the DVIEW command. Type DVIEW.

❖ **Command:**DVIEW
Select objects:
type **C** for crossing, place a window around the entire kitchen, and press **[ENTER].**
*Camera/TArget/Distance/POints/PAn/
Zoom/TWist/CLip/Hide/Off/Undo/<eXit>:*
type **TWIST [ENTER]**

Now, using the pointing device, "**twist**" the view around.

AutoCAD prompts:

New view twist<0.00> :

type **10 [ENTER]**for "**New view twist**".

The drawing should look like this (Fig. 3-24).

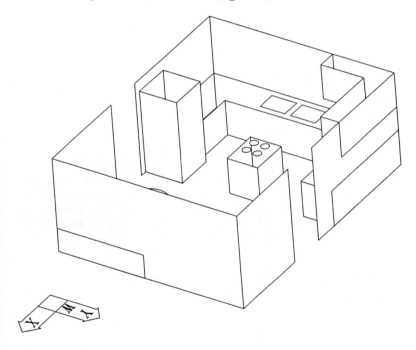

Figure 3-24 New twist angle.

Exit the DVIEW command by pressing **[ENTER].**

*Camera/TArget/Distance/POints/PAn/
Zoom/TWist/CLip/Hide/Off/Undo/<eXit>:*
press **[ENTER]**

CLIPPING THE VIEW

The **CLIP** option in **DVIEW** can be used to "peel" away sections of the rotated view. It is like "cutting" a plane through the view at a given point. Try the CLIP option.

Restore the view called **"view3"** with the VIEW command. Type VIEW.

❖ **Command:**VIEW
?/Delete/Restore/Save/Window:
type **Restore [ENTER]**
View name to restore:
type **view3 [ENTER]**

Enter the **DVIEW** command again and use the **CLIP** option. Type DVIEW.

❖ **Command:**DVIEW
Select objects:
type **C** for crossing, place a window around the entire kitchen, and press **[ENTER].**
Camera/TArget/Distance/POints/PAn
/Zoom/TWist/CLip/Hide/Off/Undo/<eXit>:
type **CLIP [ENTER]**
Back/Front/<OFF>:
type **FRONT [ENTER]**
Eye/OFF/ON/distance from target<50'-0">:

At this point, **move** the **circle** in the **scroll bar** at the top of the screen from left to right to "clip" the front of the drawing. As you move the pointing device in the scroll bar from the far left to the right, the front of the drawing will begin to disappear. "**Pick**" a point on the scroll bar (at about the middle) with the pointing device. You can use clipping planes in both parallel and perspective projections (Fig. 3-25). Examples of front clipping and back clipping are shown in Figs. 3-26 and 3-27. You can use the HIDE command to get a better view. Type **HIDE.**

Camera/TArget/Distance/POints/PAn/
Zoom/TWist/CLip/Hide/Off/Undo/<eXit>:
type **HIDE [ENTER]**

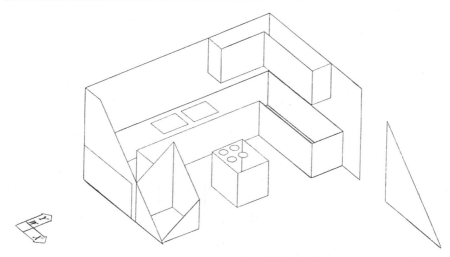

Figure 3-25 Front clipping.

The **BACK** option can be used to **CLIP the back** of the drawing off.

The **OFF** option is used to turn the **clipping** function **OFF**.

Try the **BACK** option while inside the DVIEW command.

If you exit the DVIEW command here, the drawing will remain clipped. You must reenter the DVIEW command, select the objects again, then use the CLIP **OFF** option to restore the full drawing.

Figure 3-26 illustrates **BACK** clipping. Figure 3-27 illustrates **FRONT** and **BACK** clipping used together.

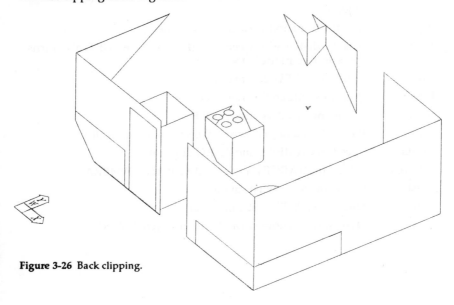

Figure 3-26 Back clipping.

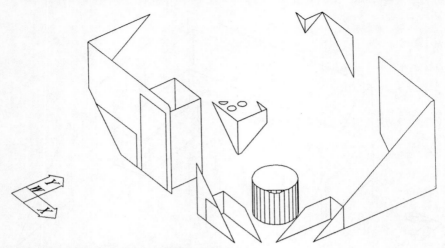

Figure 3-27 Front and back clipping together.

Exit the DVIEW command. Then exit the drawing editor and return to the AutoCAD main menu. Use the AutoCAD **QUIT** command. Type QUIT.

❖ **Command:**QUIT
   Really want to discard all changes to drawing?
   Type **Yes,** then press **[ENTER]**.

DVIEW SUMMARY

The following is a summary of all the **DVIEW** options and their functions.

Camera	Sets the CAMERA angle relative to the TARGET (selected objects)
Clip	Sets the front and back clipping planes
Distance	Sets the distance between CAMERA and TARGET, also turns **"perspective mode" ON**
eXit	Exits the DVIEW command
Hide	Performs hidden line removal
Off	Turns **"perspective mode" OFF**
PAn	Pans selected objects across the screen dynamically
POints	Specifies CAMERA and TARGET points
TARGET	Selects the TARGET angle relative to the CAMERA
TWist	Creates a view "twist" angle
Undo	**Undoes** a DVIEW subcommand
Zoom	Dynamically **zooms** in and out on selected objects

If you select **CLIP**, the following options are available:

Back	Sets the back clipping plane
Front	Sets the front clipping plane
Off	Turns "clipping" off

USING MULTIPLE VIEWPORTS

VPORTS COMMAND

The **VPORTS** (viewports) command will split the screen into as many as four screens. This gives you the opportunity to view a drawing several different ways at the same time. AutoCAD command operations can be done within each individual viewport. Different sections of a drawing can be displayed in different viewports at different angles. The advantages of using multiple viewports were illustrated in Chap. 2 and will be shown again here. Below is an example of displaying the drawing "MODEL" from Chap. 2, with four separate viewports. Each viewport displays the object from a different "viewpoint" (Fig. 3-28).

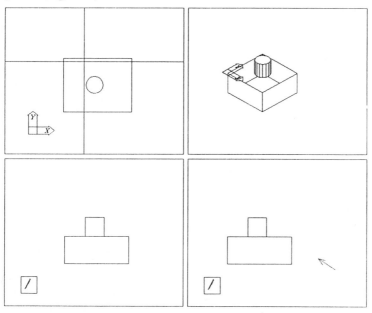

Figure 3-28 Four viewports.

The **FRONT, TOP,** and **RIGHT SIDE** views are displayed along with a pictorial view of the **MODEL**.

The **UCS icon** is only displayed in two of the viewports, indicating that you can only draw in those viewports. A **"broken pencil"** icon is displayed in the other viewports, indicating that you are not allowed to draw in those view-ports. The "broken pencil" icon means that although you may select points in that view, the X-Y plane is into the screen and selecting points in that view may be useless.

Try using the VPORTS command with the drawing you created in Chap. 2. From the AutoCAD Main Menu select **2 "Edit an EXISTING Drawing"**. Bring up the drawing called **"MODEL"**.

To **split** the screen into multiple viewports, you can activate the **VPORTS** command from the pull-down windows or type VPORTS at the command prompt line. Select the DISPLAY option from the pull-down windows. Then select **Set Viewports**. Next, select the option in the lower left corner of the dialogue box, indicating four **viewports** by placing the **arrow** in the **ACTION BOX** to the left of your selection and then "picking" with the pointing device.

To you use the VPORTS command from the keyboard simply type VPORTS and type in one of the options listed in the command prompt line.

❖ **Command:**VPORTS
   Save/Restore/Delete/Join/Single/?/2/<3>/4:
   type **4 [ENTER]**

The options are:

S   Saves a viewport configuration with a name (you may want to use names such as VP1, VP2).

R   Restores a saved viewport configuration (viewport configurations can be restored at any time and will reflect all changes made).

D   Deletes a saved viewport configuration.

J   Joins one or more viewports together.

SI   Restores to a single viewport screen.

?   Lists the saved viewport configurations.

2   Divides the current view port into two viewports.

3   Divides the current view port into three viewports.

4   Divides the current view port into four viewports.

Although you can only work in one viewport at a time, you can manipulate your viewpoint in each of the "viewports" any way you like. You can also draw from one viewport to another by changing to another viewport while you are in the middle of a command. For example, you can draw a line from one viewport to another by first entering the LINE command and picking a start point in one viewport and then activating another viewport (while still in the line command) and then picking the second point of the line in another viewport.

To activate a viewport, move the arrow into the viewport you wish to work in and **"pick"** with the pointing device (Fig. 3-28). The active viewport will be the one with the "crosshairs". You can perform any AutoCAD command within the active viewport. You can also change the way the **MODEL** is displayed in the active viewport with any of the AutoCAD 3D display commands.

Make the "upper left viewport" the active viewport by positioning the pointing device in that viewport and then "picking". Use the **PLAN** command to get a PLAN view of the "top" of the model. Type PLAN.

❖ **Command:**PLAN
  <Current UCS>/Ucs/World:
  press **[ENTER]**

Now use the ZOOM command with the **A** (all) option to view the entire limits of the drawing in the viewport. Type ZOOM.

❖ **Command:**ZOOM
  All/Center/Dynamic/Extents/
  Left/Prev/Window/<Scale(X)>:
  type **A [ENTER]**

You must also be aware of what **UCS** is active when drawing or changing your display in the active viewport. Remember, **do not** attempt to draw in a viewport if a "**broken pencil**" icon appears in the viewport. This indicates that you are not on the correct plane or **UCS**.

Each viewport can have different settings such as **GRID, SNAP, ORTHO,** or **UCS.**

To return to single viewport, first decide which of the viewports you would like to see as a full screen, then select it to make it the active viewport. Then use the **VPORTS** command with the **SI** (single) option.

If you divide a single viewport into **two** viewports, you will be prompted to select either a **horizontal** or **vertical** split. The **AXIS** tick marks can only be used if you have a single viewport.

☞   NOTE: Only one viewport can be activated at a time. Commands will only effect the current viewport.

REDRAWALL AND REGENALL

You will notice that at times there will be parts of the drawing in one or more viewports erased from the screen while editing. The **REDRAW** and **REGEN** commands will **only** redraw the **active viewport.**

You must use the **REDRAWALL** command to redraw all the viewports on the screen. The **REGENALL** command will regenerate all the viewports on the screen. Regenerating a drawing with the REGENALL command will be much more time consuming with multiple viewports than using the REGEN command with a single viewport.

These commands are located under the **DISPLAY** option in the screen menu or can be typed in at the command prompt line.

Let's try the **REDRAWALL** command from the command prompt line. Type REDRAWALL.

❖ **Command:**REDRAWALL

Exit the AutoCAD drawing editor without saving this drawing. Use the **QUIT** command.

❖ **Command:**QUIT
Really want to discard all changes to drawing?
Type **Yes**, then press **[ENTER]**

SUMMARY

Changing your viewpoint of a model with the 3D display commands gives you the flexibility to rotate the drawing around on the screen so you can draw on any side. However, before you start drawing on a particular side you will need to define a plane or User Coordinate System (UCS) to draw on as shown in Chap. 2.

Chapter 4 will fully explain the UCS command and all of its options for defining User Coordinate Systems to work in. Each UCS can have its own distinct origin location and X and Y axis directions.

The UCSICON command, which is used to position the display of the UCS icon on the screen, will also be discussed.

USER COORDINATE SYSTEMS

UCS

U p until AutoCAD Release 10 there was only one plane on which to work, the **X-Y plane**. This is referred to as the "cartesian coordinate system", or the "**World Coordinate System**" (WCS) indicated by the **WCS** icon at the bottom left corner of the AutoCAD drawing editor.

The World Coordinate System defines the lower left corner of the drawing editor as the drawing origin (0,0) with the X axis being horizontal and the Y axis being vertical. **User Coordinate Systems** (UCS) are similar to the World Coordinate System except that they are defined by the user. You can define a new origin or multiple origins and a new X-Y axis orientation anywhere in three-dimensional space.

User Coordinate Systems can be regarded as separate planes to work in and are used to change the drawing origin and axes to facilitate drawing construction. Several user coordinate systems can be defined, but you are limited to working in only one at a time.

User Coordinate Systems are used for three-dimensional drawings but can also be used for 2D drawing applications.

The figure below (Fig. 4-1) shows the WCS and UCS icons, which are usually displayed at the lower left corner of the AutoCAD drawing editor. A "W" in the icon indicates that you are currently working in the **World** Coordinate System. A "+" in the UCS icon indicates that you are currently working in a **user**-defined coordinate system.

Whichever icon is displayed is considered the **current** coordinate system, or **current UCS**. All coordinate input and display will be relative to the current UCS.

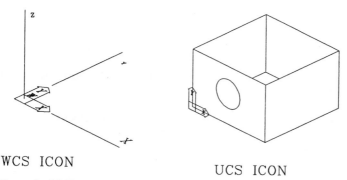

WCS ICON   UCS ICON

Figure 4-1 WCS and UCS icons.

The following characteristics can be defined or changed for all User Coordinate Systems in a drawing:

- New origin
- New X, Y, Z axes directions
- New rotation for the current UCS around any of its axes

X-Y-Z COORDINATES

All coordinate systems also have a "Z axis" in addition to their X and Y axes to use for the third dimension of **height**, or **thickness**. The Z axis is defined by the "right hand rule" described earlier as perpendicular to the X-Y plane. Below is a representation of the X-Y-Z axes for the World Coordinate System (Fig. 4-2).

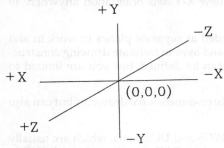

Figure 4-2 X-Y-Z axes.

SETTING UP TO DRAW WITH UCS

To create separate planes, or User Coordinate Systems (UCS), we will use the UCS command. Let's follow the example below. First begin a new drawing and name it **UCS**.

Use the following drawing parameters:

UNITS

ENGINEERING	3
Number of digits to right of Dec.	4
Systems of angle measurement	2 (Degrees / minutes / seconds)
Number of fractional places for display of angles:	4
Direction for angle 0d0':	0d0' (East 3 o'clock)
Angles measure clockwise?:	No

LIMITS

Lower left:	0,0
Upper right:	34, 22

GRID

X spacing	= 1
Y spacing	= 1

SNAP

X spacing	= 1
Y spacing	= 1

If you are not experienced with AutoCAD and do not know how to start a drawing using the UNITS and LIMITS commands, follow the procedure outlined here. The [ENTER] key can be used to select AutoCAD default values.

1. From the AutoCAD main menu select item **1, Begin a NEW drawing.**

2. Name the drawing **"UCS".**

3. From the command prompt line enter the **UNITS** command:

   ❖ **Command:**UNITS

The following is displayed:

System of units:	(Examples)
1. Scientific	1.55E+01
2. Decimal	15.50
3. Engineering	1'-3.50"
4. Architectural	1'-3 1/2"
5. Fractional	15 1/2

Enter choice, 1 to 5<default> :
type **3 [ENTER]**
Number of digits to right of
decimal point (0 to 8) <default> :
type **2 [ENTER]**

The UNITS command proceeds to angles and displays the following menu:

Systems of angle measure	Examples
1. Decimal degrees	45.0000
2. Degrees/minutes/seconds	45d0'0"
3. Grads	50.0000g
4. Radians	0.7854r
5. Surveyor's units	N 45d0'0" E

Enter choice, 1 to 5 <default>:
type **2 [ENTER]**

Number of fractional places for display of angles (0 to 8) <default> :
type **4 [ENTER]**

After selecting the angle format, the following prompt will appear:

Direction for angle 0:

East	3 o'clock	= 0
North	12 o'clock	= 90
West	9 o'clock	= 180
South	6 o'clock	= 270

Enter direction for angle <0 d0'0">:
press **[ENTER]**

After selecting the angle 0 direction, you'll receive the prompt:

Do you want angles measured clockwise <N>:
press **[ENTER]**

Pressing **[ENTER]** will select the AutoCAD defaults. The defaults indicate that AutoCAD will measure angles in a counterclockwise direction with 0 degrees being due **east** or at 3 o'clock.

4. Next you should set the **LIMITS**. Enter the LIMITS command:

❖ **Command:**LIMITS
ON/OFF/<lower left corner><0 '-0.00",0'-0.00">:
press **[ENTER]** for lower left corner
Upper right corner <1'-0.00",0'-9.00">:
type **34,22 [ENTER]**

5. Set the GRID size to 1. Type **GRID**.

❖ **Command:**GRID
Grid spacing(X) or ON/OFF/Snap/Aspect <0'-0.00">:
type **1 [ENTER]**

6. Set the **SNAP** to 1. Type **SNAP**.

❖ **Command:**SNAP
Snap spacing or ON/OFF/Aspect/Rotate/Style <0'-1.00">:
type **1 [ENTER]**

Make sure the **GRIDS** are **ON [F7]** and use the **ZOOM** command with the **A** (all) option to get the full drawing limits shown on the screen.

7. Enter the ZOOM command.

❖ **Command:**ZOOM
All/Center/Dynamic/Extents/
Left/Prev/Window/<Scale(X)>:
type **A [ENTER]**

This allows you to view the entire limits of the drawing on the screen.

DRAWING THE MODEL

Follow the procedure outlined here to create a 3D model and manipulate AutoCAD's User Coordinate Systems so you can draw on its faces.

With the **LINE** command draw a 12- by 12-inch square in the WCS as shown below (Fig. 4-3).

Figure 4-3 12- by 12-inch square.

Enter the **CHANGE** command and give the square a **thickness** of **12**.

❖ **Command:**CHANGE
Select objects:
pick all four sides of the square, then **[ENTER]**
Properties/<Change point>:
type **P [ENTER]**
Change what Property (Color/Elev/LAyer
/LType/Thickness)?:
type **TH** for thickness **[ENTER]**
New Thickness <0'-0.00">:
type **12 [ENTER]**
press **[ENTER]** to exit CHANGE command.

Enter the **DVIEW** command to rotate the object:

❖ **Command:**DVIEW
Select objects:
type **C** for crossing and place a window around the entire square, then **[ENTER]**

Camera/TArget/Distance/POints/PAn
/Zoom/TWist/CLip/Hide/Off/Undo/<eXit>:
type **CAmera [ENTER]**
Enter angle from X-Y plane<90.00>:
type **35 [ENTER]**
Enter angle in X-Y plane from X axis<-90.00>:
type **35 [ENTER]**

You should still be in the DVIEW command.

Camera/TArget/Distance/POints/PAn
/Zoom/TWist/CLip/Hide/Off/Undo/<eXit>:
press **[ENTER]**

This will **exit** you from the **DVIEW** command. You should now have a view
of the cube that looks like this (Fig. 4-4):

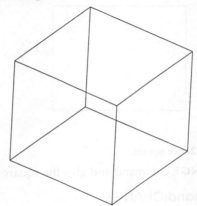

Figure 4-4 Cube.

Save this view with the **VIEW** command as **V1**.

❖ **Command:**VIEW
?/Delete/Restore/Save/Window:
type **Save [ENTER]**
View name to save:
type **V1 [ENTER]**

CONTROLLING THE UCS ICON

Now we are almost ready to set up separate **User Coordinate Systems** (planes)
to draw on. But first we will set up the way the **UCS icon** will appear on the
screen.

You will notice that the UCS icon will appear at different locations on the screen
when you change your viewpoint. Usually it will be displayed at the lower left
corner of the drawing editor.

As you change from one UCS to another you may want to display the position of the **icon** at its new origin location. To do this we need to tell AutoCAD where the new UCS icons should appear in the drawing. From the command prompt line enter the **UCSICON** command.

❖ **Command:**UCSICON
   ON/OFF/All/Noorigin/ORigin/ <current ON/OFF state>:
   type **A [ENTER]**

This will ensure that the icons will be changed in all viewports as we move from one UCS to another. Next AutoCAD prompts:

ON/OFF/All/Noorigin/ORigin/-ON>:
   type **OR [ENTER]**

Notice that the icon jumps to the top left of the drawing limits.

This will ensure that every UCS created will have the icon appear at its defined origin location. The UCS command options are described below.

ON   Turns the UCS icon display on

OFF   Turns the UCS icon display off

A(All) Makes the changes to the UCS icons active in all viewports

N   Always display the icon at the lower left corner of the viewport
       (Noorigin)

OR   Forces the icon to display at the origin of the current UCS

☞   **NOTE:** The UCSICON command only controls the **display** of the UCS
           icons.

SEPARATING PLANES

Reduce the display of the drawing down with the ZOOM command to a size so that the whole drawing fits in the center of the screen (Fig. 4-5). Type ZOOM.

❖ **Command:**ZOOM
   All/Center/Dynamic/Extents/
   Left/Prev/Window/<Scale(X)>:
   type **.7x [ENTER]**

Now create a new **User Coordinate System.** Enter the UCS command:

❖ **Command:**UCS
   Origin/Zaxis/3point/Entity/View/
   X/Y/Z/Prev/Restore/Save/Del/?/<World>:
   type **3Point [ENTER]**
   Origin point<0 ,0,0>:
   type **INT [ENTER]**
   INTERSEC of

pick **P1**
Point on positive portion of X-axis<0,0,0>:
type **INT [ENTER]**
INTERSEC of
pick **P2**
Point on positive-Y portion of the UCS X-Y plane<0,0,0>:
type **INT [ENTER]**
INTERSEC of
pick **P3**

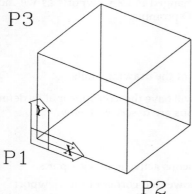

Figure 4-5 FRONT User Coordinate System (UCS).

GRID and **SNAP** can be turned **OFF** at this point.

Re-enter the **UCS** command by pressing the **[ENTER]** key and **"save"** this new UCS.

❖ **Command:**UCS
Origin/Zaxis/3point/Entity/View/
X/Y/Z/Prev/Restore/Save/Del/?/<World>:
type **Save [ENTER]**
?/Name of UCS:
type **FRONT [ENTER]**

You have now defined and saved a new plane, or UCS, in which to draw in called **FRONT**. All drawing entities drawn while this UCS is active will be relative to its defined origin and X, Y, and Z axes orientation.

Use the MODIFY LAYER option under SETTINGS in the pull-down windows to define a new **LAYER** called **MODEL** with a **color** of **cyan** and make the layer **current**. Now enter the **LINE** command and draw a line from point **P1** to **P2** in the middle of the FRONT view as shown in Fig. 4-6. Use the **MID**point OSNAP tool to snap to the midpoint of each line. Press **[ENTER]** to exit the LINE command.

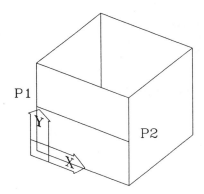

Figure 4-6 Drawing on the FRONT UCS.

Re-enter the **UCS** command to create the **UCS** for the **"right side view"** (Fig. 4-7). Type UCS.

❖ **Command:**UCS
Origin/Zaxis/3point/Entity/View/
X/Y/Z/Prev/Restore/Save/Del/?/<World>:
type **OR [ENTER]**
Origin point<0 ,0,0>:
type **INT [ENTER]**
INTERSEC of
pick **P2**

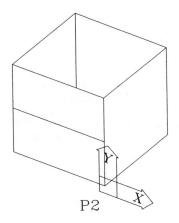

Figure 4-7 Positioning the UCS icon.

Re-enter the UCS command by pressing the [ENTER] key.

❖ **Command:**UCS
Origin/Zaxis/3point/Entity/View/
X/Y/Z/Prev/Restore/Save/Del/?/<World>:
type **Y [ENTER]**
Rotation angle about Y axis<0.0> :
type **90 [ENTER]**

The UCS icon should look like the one shown below (Fig. 4-8):

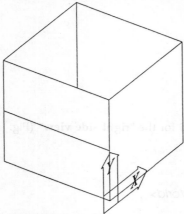

Figure 4-8 Right side UCS.

Re-enter the UCS command by pressing the [ENTER] key and **"save"** this UCS.

❖ **Command:**UCS
Origin/Zaxis/3point/Entity/View/
X/Y/Z/Prev/Restore/Save/Del/?/<World>:
type save **[ENTER]**
?/Name of UCS:
type **RIGHT [ENTER]**

You have now created the **right side** plane. This UCS has an origin at the lower left corner on the right side of the cube and has been named "RIGHT".

Draw a circle with the **CIRCLE** command in the right side view close to the center with a small radius and use the **CHANGE** command to assign a **thickness** of 3 to the circle.

❖ **Command:**CHANGE
Select objects:
pick the **circle,** then **[ENTER]**
Properties/<Change point>:
type **P [ENTER]**

*Change what Property (Color/Elev/LAyer/
LType/Thickness)?:*
type **TH** for thickness **[ENTER]**
New Thickness <0'-0.00">:
type **3 [ENTER]**
press **[ENTER]** to **exit** the CHANGE command.

Notice the direction of the **thickness,** or **"Z axis"**, in this UCS (Fig. 4-9).

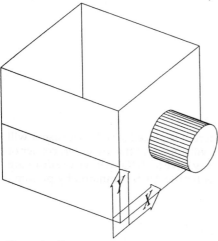

Figure 4-9 Thickness in side view.

Enter the **UCS** command again to create the **"top view"** (Fig. 4-10). Type UCS.

❖ **Command:**UCS
*Origin/Zaxis/3point/Entity/View/
X/Y/Z/Prev/Restore/Save/Del/?/<World>:*
type **OR [ENTER]**
Origin point <0,0,0>:
type **INT [ENTER]**
INTERSEC of
pick **P1**

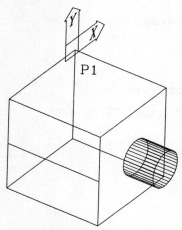

Figure 4-10 Positioning the UCS icon in the TOP view.

Occasionally the icon will not appear where it is placed simply because it will not fit on the screen. In this case the icon will appear at the lower left corner of the screen at the correct orientation. You may have to ZOOM down the drawing to see the icon in its proper position. Re-enter the **UCS** command by pressing **[ENTER]**.

❖ **Command:**UCS
Origin/Zaxis/3point/Entity/View/
X/Y/Z/Prev/Restore/Save/Del/?/<World>:
type **X [ENTER]**
Rotation angle about X axis <0.0>:
type **-90 [ENTER]**

Notice the direction of the UCS icon now (Fig. 4-11).

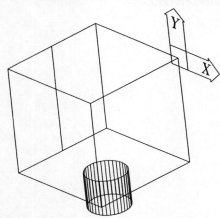

Figure 4-11 Rotating the UCS icon.

Re-enter the **UCS** command by pressing **[ENTER]**.

❖ **Command:**UCS
Origin/Zaxis/3point/Entity/View/
X/Y/Z/Prev/Restore/Save/Del/?/<World>:
type **Z [ENTER]**
Rotation angle about Z axis<0.0>:
type **180 [ENTER]**

The new UCS icon should be correctly positioned as follows (Fig. 4-12):

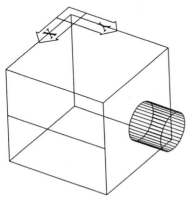

Figure 4-12 TOP view User Coordinate System (UCS).

Re-enter the **UCS** command by pressing the **[ENTER]** key and **"save"** this UCS.

❖ **Command:**UCS
Origin/Zaxis/3point/Entity/View/
X/Y/Z/Prev/Restore/Save/Del/?/<World>:
type **Save [ENTER]**
?/Name of UCS:
type **TOP [ENTER]**

Three separate User Coordinate Systems (**UCS**) have now been created. Each has a separate name and its own distinct origin and X, Y, and Z axes orientation.

Draw a line with the **LINE** command through the middle of the top view from point **P1** to point **P2** as shown in Fig. 4-13 (use MIDpoint OSNAP tool). Then draw a line from the **endpoint** of the line you just drew in the top view to the **endpoint** of the line in the front view (use the **OSNAP** tool **END**point). Then copy the line to the back plane. The drawing should look like Fig. 4-13 on the next page.

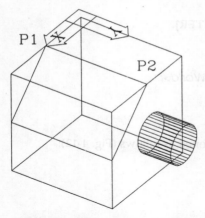

Figure 4-13 Drawing from one UCS to another.

3DFACE COMMAND

Draw a **3DFACE** with the 3DFACE command in the **top view**. The **3DFACE** command can be accessed by selecting **3D** from the root screen menu. Enter the **3DFACE** command and pick the following points as shown (Fig. 4-14):

❖ **Command:**3DFACE
First point:
type **INT [ENTER]**
INTERSEC of
pick **P1**
Second point:
type **INT [ENTER]**
INTERSEC of
pick **P2**
Third point:
type **INT [ENTER]**
INTERSEC of
pick **P3**
Fourth point:
type **INT [ENTER]**
INTERSEC of
pick **P4**
Third point:
press **[ENTER]** to exit the **3DFACE** command.

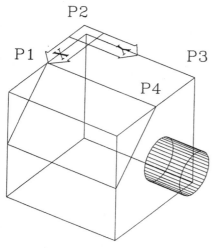

Figure 4-14 Drawing a 3DFACE.

The **3DFACE** command creates a **solid** surface on an object. The 3DFACE command is similar to the SOLID command but, unlike the SOLID command, points are selected in a clockwise or counterclockwise direction, not across the diagonal. Use the **Invisible** option preceding the first point of that edge to make an edge of a 3DFACE invisible when viewed as a wireframe. The **Invisible** option is used to hide an edge of a 3DFACE.

While still in the active UCS called "TOP", draw **3DFACES** all around the sides of the object, on the bottom square, the back square, the inclined surface, and the small rectangle in the front view as shown in Fig. 4-15. The faces are 2, 3, 4, and 5.

☞ **NOTE:** You must use the **object snap tools** to capture the **ENDpoints or INTersections** when drawing from plane to plane in different UCSs. Use a running INTersection OSNAP to pick each corner. You may also have to restore the World Coordinate System (WCS) before drawing the 3DFACES.

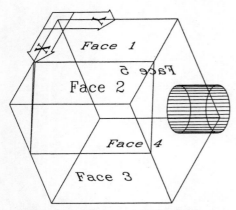

Figure 4-15 Drawing 3DFACES around the model.

Save this view with the **VIEW** command as **V2**.

❖ **Command:**VIEW
  ?/Delete/Restore/Save/Window:
  type **Save [ENTER]**
  View name to save:
  type **V2 [ENTER]**

Now turn the **LAYER 0 OFF** with the MODIFY LAYER dialogue box activated from the pull-down windows under SETTINGS. The model should look like Fig. 4-16.

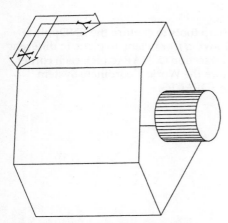

Figure 4-16 3D model with 3DFACES.

Now create a UCS on the **inclined surface**. Enter the **UCS** command.

❖ **Command:**UCS
   Origin/Zaxis/3point/Entity/View/
   X/Y/Z/Prev/Restore/Save/Del/?/<World>:
   type **3Point [ENTER]**
   Origin point<0,0,0>:
   type **INT [ENTER]**
   INTERSEC of
   pick **P1**
   Point on positive portion of X-axis<0,0,0>:
   type **INT [ENTER]**
   INTERSEC of
   pick **P2**
   Point on positive-Y portion of the UCS X-Y plane<0,0,0>:
   type **INT [ENTER]**
   INTERSEC of
   pick **P3**

Notice the direction of the crosshairs and the icon. The object looks like Fig. 4-17:

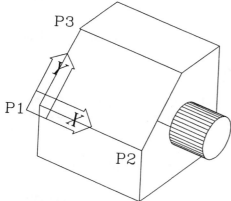

Figure 4-17 UCS on inclined surface.

Re-enter the **UCS** command by pressing the **[ENTER]** key and **"save"** this UCS.

❖ **Command:**UCS
   Origin/Zaxis/3point/Entity/View/
   X/Y/Z/Prev/Restore/Save/Del/?/<World>:
   type **save [ENTER]**
   ?/Name of UCS:
   type **FACE2 [ENTER]**

Draw a circle with a small radius on the inclined surface (FACE2).

The drawing now looks like the one in Fig. 4-18 on the next page.

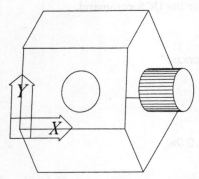

Figure 4-18 Drawing on the inclined surface.

Save the drawing with the **SAVE** command.

❖ **Command:**SAVE
File name <UCS> :
press **[ENTER]**

UCS COMMAND SUMMARY

You have now used most of the UCS subcommands with this example. All of the UCS options are listed and defined here:

Origin/Zaxis/3point/Entity/View/X/Y/Z/Prev/
Restore/Save/Del/?/<World>:

O (Origin)   Defines a new UCS by establishing a new origin (X,Y,Z). The origin can be selected with the pointing device or typed at the keyboard.

Origin point<0 ,0,0>:   (enter new point)

ZA (ZAxis)   Defines a new Z axis angle. The X-Y plane will adjust perpendicular to the new plane.

3Point   Picks three points to define a new UCS and plane. The origin is selected, then the positive X direction and then the positive Y direction.

E (Entity)   Defines a UCS by selecting an existing entity in a drawing. The new UCS is aligned with the selected entity with respect to the UCS in which the entity was created.

V (View)   Defines a new UCS which is parallel to your viewing direction. Sets X as horizontal and Y as vertical, looking directly at the screen.

X/Y/Z   Rotates the current UCS around one of the axes.

P (Previous) Restores the previously saved UCS.

R (Restore) Restores a saved UCS by name.

S (Save)   Saves a UCS by name.

D (Delete)   Deletes a saved UCS.

?   Lists all saved UCS.

W (World)   Restores the World Coordinate System (**WCS**). This is the UCS command default.

☞ **NOTE:** If the UCS is set to appear at the origin locations with the UCSICON command and the object does not fit on the screen, the UCS icon will appear at the lower left corner of the drawing editor or current viewport.

RESTORING A SAVED UCS

To restore a previously saved **UCS** use the **Restore** option. Enter the UCS command and restore the **front** UCS.

❖ **Command:**UCS
Origin/Zaxis/3point/Entity/View/
X/Y/Z/Prev/Restore/Save/Del/?/<World>:
type **R [ENTER]**
?/Name of UCS to restore:
type **FRONT [ENTER]**

The UCS icon should now be positioned as shown below (Fig. 4-19):

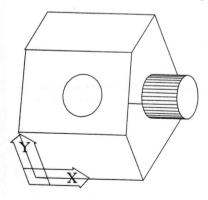

Figure 4-19 Restoring the FRONT UCS.

To **list** all the "**saved**" UCSs use the **?** option. Enter the **UCS** command.

❖ **Command:**UCS
Origin/Zaxis/3point/Entity/View/
X/Y/Z/Prev/Restore/Save/Del/?/<World>:
type **R [ENTER]**
?/Name of UCS:
type **? [ENTER]**

Figure 4-20 shows AutoCAD displays:

FRONT

Origin =<6.9927,4.8901,0.0000>,   X Axis =<0.0000 ,1.0000,0.0000>
Y Axis =<0.0000,0.0000,1.0000>,   Z Axis =<1.0000 ,0.0000,-0.0000>

RIGHT

Origin =<6.9927,5.9638,0.0000>,   X Axis = <-1.0000,0.0000,0.0000>
Y Axis =<0.0000,0.0000,1.0000>,   Z Axis =<0.0000 ,1.0000,0.0000>

TOP

Origin =<6.4558,4.8901,1.0738>,   X Axis =< -0.0000,1.0000,-0.0000>
Y Axis =< -1.0000,-0.0000,-0.0000>, Z Axis =<-0.0000,0.0000,1.0000>

FACE2

Origin =<6.9927,4.8901,0.5369>,   X Axis =<0.0000 ,1.0000,0.0000>
Y Axis =< -0.7057,0.0000,0.7085>, Z Axis =<0.7085 ,0.0000,0.7057>

Figure 4-20 Listing the User Coordinate Systems.

press [ENTER] to exit the UCS command.

UCS VIEW OPTION

You can add **text** to the 3D drawing on any of the UCSs or you can set the text parallel to the screen. Use the **UCS** command with the **View** option to set the UCS parallel to the screen. Enter the UCS command.

❖ **Command:**UCS
Origin/Zaxis/3point/Entity/View/
X/Y/Z/Prev/Restore/Save/Del/?/<World>:
type **View [ENTER]**

This will cause the UCS to appear in the lower left corner of the origin with the X-Y plane parallel to the screen, as shown in Fig. 4-21 . It does not matter how the object is orientated.

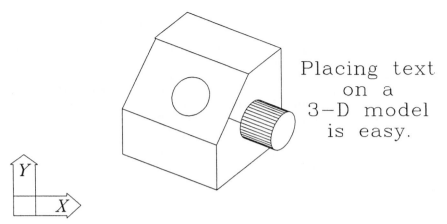

Placing text
on a
3-D model
is easy.

Figure 4-21 UCS "View" option for placing text.

Add the text as shown with the TEXT command.

❖ **Command:**DTEXT
Start point or Align/
Center/Fit/Middle/Right/Style:
pick start point
Height <0'-.20">:
type 1 **[ENTER]**
Rotation angle <0d0'0">:
press **[ENTER]**
Text:
type a line of text, then **[ENTER]**
Text:
Continue to type text, **[ENTER]** when complete.

UCS DIALOGUE BOX

The UCS commands can be activated and controlled by the **UCS dialogue box.**
Select SETTINGS from the pull-down windows at the top of the screen. Scroll
down and select **UCS DIALOGUE....**

Notice that the User Coordinate Systems that we saved all appear here. To
change from one UCS to another simply move the checkmark under the column
"current" to the UCS you want to work in, then select **OK.** The UCS icon will
change positions on the drawing.

You can also use the dialogue box to define new or rename existing User
Coordinate Systems. To rename a User Coordinate System simply move the
arrow pointer over the box that has the UCS name you want to change, when
it becomes highlighted, type a new name. A **checkmark** placed in the **current**
box will restore that particular UCS.

The **LIST** option will list the coordinate settings for a specified UCS.

To define a new UCS, activate the UCS dialogue box from the pull-down window again, and select **Define new current UCS** from the bottom of the dialogue box. From the next dialogue box select the **UCS name** box and type a **new UCS name**; then select a desired option from the list. The new UCS is defined relative to the current UCS. Remember to make it **current** by placing a checkmark next to it under the column for **current**.

Use the **END** command to exit the AutoCAD drawing editor and save the drawing. Below is the UCS dialogue box (Fig. 4-22).

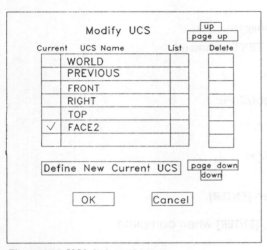

Figure 4-22 UCS dialogue box.

SUMMARY

The commands used up to this point will allow you to create basic 3D models without any curves to them.

Occasionally you will need to design more complex 3D shapes. Chapter 5 will introduce you to more advanced 3D commands to create 3D meshes.

The 3DPOLY, 3DMESH, RULESURF, TABSURF, REVSURF, EDGESURF, and SETVAR commands will be discussed.

CHAPTER FIVE

3D SURFACE MODELS

B efore drawing the previous 3D models, we first established the overall size of the model by defining its length and width in the X-Y plane. The boundaries of the model were created with the **LINE** command in the World Coordinate System and a **thick**ness was then assigned to the lines. The 3D object was then viewed from a different angle with the **DVIEW** or **VPOINT** command to visualize the actual model. This representation is called a "3D **wireframe**" model. The model is actually transparent; there are no actual surfaces on the model.

AutoCAD offers a set of 3D commands which apply surfaces to a wireframe model. The following pages will discuss the procedure for using these commands.

3D LINES AND FACES

In previous versions of AutoCAD the 3DLINE command was used to draw lines in 3D space. With AutoCAD Release 10, the **LINE** command has **replaced** the **3DLINE** command and has been altered to allow you to draw lines on any plane, or User Coordinate System. The Z coordinate has also been added.

The **3DFACE** command is the first of the surface modeling commands.

The **3DFACE** command was used in Chap. 4 to add flat **sol**id surfaces to the existing model. The 3DFACE command can be used to create faces on a wireframe model in any UCS to give the model "surfaces" that can be later shaded with AutoCAD's rendering program AutoSHADE.

The commands discussed to this point were used to create basic 3D models that are flat on all planes with no curves. To create more complex 3D models with curved surfaces, the **3DFACE** and LINE commands are not sufficient. This Chapter will discuss the advanced AutoCAD 3D commands used to create more complex 3D shapes.

All of the AutoCAD 3D commands can be accessed from the **3D** option in the root screen menu, from the **Draw** pull-down window **(3D Construction...)**, or from the template section labeled **3D/AUTOSHADE**.

3D POLYLINES

The second of the more complex 3D commands is the **3DPOLY** command.

The **3DPOLY** command creates a three dimensional polyline consisting of all straight line segments in three-dimensional space. This command is very much similar to the **PLINE** command. Three dimensional polylines are polylines drawn from one plane to another, or from one UCS to another.

Let's use the **3DPOLY** command to create a three-dimensional polyline.

From the AutoCAD **main menu** select **1, Begin a NEW drawing.** Name the drawing anything you like. Once AutoCAD has been loaded and you are in the drawing editor, press **[F7]** to turn the **GRIDS ON.**

Now change your angle of view with the **VPOINT** command. Type VPOINT.

> ❖ **Command:**VPOINT
> *Rotate/<view point><0.000,0.000,0.000>:*
> type **1,-1,1 [ENTER]**

Now **ZOOM** the drawing down to view the entire **limits** at this angle using the **ZOOM** command.

> ❖ **Command:**ZOOM
> *All/Center/Dynamic/Extents/*
> *Left/Prev/Window/<Scale(X)>:*
> type **.7 [ENTER]**

☞   **NOTE:** The GRID boundaries indicate the drawing **limits.**

PAN the drawing to the center of the screen if necessary.

Draw the 3D polyline shown below (Fig. 5-1) using the **3DPOLY** command. Select the **3D** option from the root screen menu, then the **3DPOLY** command. Or type **3DPOLY** in at the command prompt line.

> ❖ **Command:***3DPOLY*
> *From point:*
> type **2,2,0 [ENTER]**
> *Close/Undo/<Endpoint of Line>:*
> type **4,2,1 [ENTER]**
> *Close/Undo/<Endpoint of Line>:*
> type **5,3,2 [ENTER]**
> *Close/Undo/<Endpoint of Line>:*
> type **3,5,3 [ENTER]**
> *Close/Undo/<Endpoint of Line>:*
> type **1,4,3 [ENTER]**
> *Close/Undo/<Endpoint of Line>:*
> type **5,2,4 [ENTER]**
> *Close/Undo/<Endpoint of Line>:*
> type **6,5,5** [ENTER]
> *Close/Undo/<Endpoint of Line>:*
> press **[ENTER]** to exit the 3DPOLY command.

This will draw a polyline consisting of one segment from point 2,2,0 to 4,2,1 to 5,3,2 to 3,5,3 to 1,4,3 to 5,2,4 to 6,5,5 in the World Coordinate System (Fig. 5-1). The 3D polyline is created in three-dimensional space and can be edited with the **PEDIT** command and viewed from different viewpoints with the **DVIEW** or **VPOINT** commands.

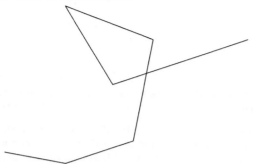

Figure 5-1 3D Polyline.

Of course if you don't give Z values, the polyline created will lie flat on the X-Y plane only. You can pick as many points as desired. If you type **"Close"** or **"C"** within the **3DPOLY** command, it will close the polyline back to the starting point of the segment or polyline, providing you have more than one segment. If you look at the 3D polyline in PLAN view, it will certainly appear much different. From the command prompt line enter the PLAN command. Type PLAN.

    ❖ **Command:**PLAN
       <Current UCS>/UCS/World:
       press **[ENTER]**

Then enter the **ZOOM** command with the **A** (all) option to view the entire drawing limits.

    ❖ **Command:**ZOOM
       All/Center/Dynamic/Extents/
       Left/Prev/Window/<Scale(X)>:
       type **A [ENTER]**

Notice how the 3D polyline appears now. Change your viewpoint back to the way it was in Fig. 5-1 with the VPOINT command. Type VPOINT.

    ❖ **Command:**VPOINT
       Rotate/<View point><0.0000,0.0000,1.000>:
       press **1,-1,1 [ENTER]**

Now **ZOOM** the drawing down to view the entire limits at this angle using the ZOOM command again.

    ❖ **Command:**ZOOM
       All/Center/Dynamic/Extents/
       Left/Prev/Window/<Scale(X)>:
       type **.7 [ENTER]**

Save the drawing at this point with SAVE command. Type SAVE.

> ❖ **Command**:SAVE
> *File name <current>:*
> press **[ENTER]**

EDITING 3D POLYLINES

The **PEDIT** command can be used to edit 3D polylines just as it edited 2D polylines. If you select the **Spline** option you will get some unique 3D effects.

Using the drawing we just created in Fig. 5-1, copy the 3D polyline with the **COPY** command to the right of the original polyline. Now edit the second polyline with the PEDIT command (Fig. 5-2). Enter the **PEDIT** command and select the second of the 3D polylines and try the **Spline** option. Type PEDIT.

> ❖ **Command**:PEDIT
> *Select polyline:*
> *Select second polyline.*
> *Close/Edit vertex/Spline curve/Decurve/Undo/eXit<X>:*
> type **Spline [ENTER]**

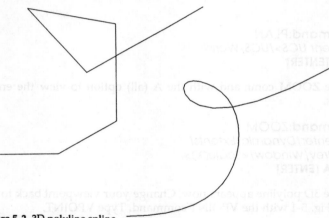

Figure 5-2 3D polyline spline.

The vertices of the 3D polyline can be edited also with the **"Edit Vertex"** option under the **PEDIT** command in the same manner as editing a 2D polyline, by moving the **"X"** located at the vertex that you want to change. From within the PEDIT command use the **Edit** vertex option to change one of the vertex points of the polyline. Type **E** for Edit vertex.

> *Close/Edit vertex/Spline curve/Decurve/Undo/eXit<X>:*
> type **E [ENTER]**

The PEDIT command issues a new set of options to choose:

Next/Previous/Break/Insert/Move/Regen/Straighten/eXit <N>:

If you press **[ENTER]** twice, you will see the "X" move up the polyline to the location of the third vertex before using the **Spline** option. The **N** option means **Next** vertex. AutoCAD prompts:

Next/Previous/Break/Insert/Move/Regen/Straighten/eXit<N>:
Type **"M"** for **move**.
Enter new location:

Pick a new location with the pointing device about three units to the right of the "X" marker for the vertex to move. Notice the change in the 3D polyline.

Now exit the PEDIT command. From the PEDIT command prompt:

Next/Previous/Break/Insert/Move/Regen/Straighten/eXit<N>:
Type **X** for eXit, then **[ENTER]**. AutoCAD prompts

Close/Edit vertex/Spline curve/Decurve/Undo/eXit<X>:
press **[ENTER]** here again to exit the PEDIT command.

Now **exit** this drawing and return to the AutoCAD main menu. Use the **END** command. Type **END**.

❖ **Command:**END

☞ **NOTE:** The AutoCAD OSNAP modes can be used to snap to geometric points of objects to accurately draw and edit from one plane to another if there are other entities in the drawing.

SURFACE MODELING COMMANDS

AutoCAD Release 10 supplies you with some other 3D commands that give some dramatic visual effects when creating more complex 3D objects.

This chapter will discuss the AutoCAD commands to create **3D surfaces,** which are referred to as "3D meshes".

The 3D commands to create meshes are defined here:

RULESURF	Creates a surface between two known objects (Ruled surfaces)
TABSURF	Extends a surface relative to the shape of an object (tabulated surfaces)
REVSURF	Creates a surface by revolving a defined shape around an axis (surfaces of revolution)
EDGESURF	Creates a surface by selecting four separate edges or sides (edge-defined surface patches)
3DMESH	Creates mesh or surface as defined by the user entering points for vertices

These commands can be accessed from the **DRAW** option in the pull-down windows under **3D construction,** from the **3D** option in the root screen menu, or from the **3D/AUTOSHADE** section of the template or they can be typed in at the keyboard.

3D POLYGON MESHES

The 3D AutoCAD commands listed above provide methods of generating 3D polygon meshes to define flat or curved surfaces.

Before we begin, let's define what a **mesh** or **surface** is. A **"mesh"** is a single entity that attempts to place **multiple 3DFACES** on the surface of an object. A mesh is defined by a simple matrix of M and N vertices as shown below (Fig. 5-3). A good analogy would be to view the mesh as a grid system with columns and rows. The **M and N** values specify the position of the vertices for the columns and rows.

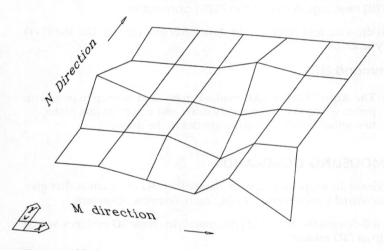

Figure 5-3 Mesh.

The **3DMESH** command allows you to specify the number of vertices in the M and the N directions and the 3D location of each vertex in the mesh. You can specify the spacing between the lines in a mesh by changing the AutoCAD system variables **SURFTAB1** and **SURFTAB2** (these variables change the distance between the columns and rows in a mesh).

SURFTAB1 controls the density of a mesh created with the **RULESURF** and **TABSURF** commands. As you will see, these are not actually cross-grids but single lines forming the mesh. SURFTAB1 controls the density of **single line meshes.**

SURFTAB2 and SURFTAB1 used together control the density of any cross-grid mesh as created with the REVSURF and EDGESURF commands. SURFTAB2 with SURFTAB1 control the density of all **cross-grid meshes**. These variables can be changed at any time and only control the density of the 3D meshes. The more dense the mesh, the slower the REDRAW or REGEN time for the drawing.

Polygon meshes can be open or closed and are used preferably when you need to draw an object as one entity. The 3DMESH command is discussed at the end of this chapter.

RULESURF COMMAND

The first of the 3D mesh commands is called RULESURF. The **RULESURF** (ruled surfaces) command is used to define a mesh or surface between two existing entities in a drawing. Let's explore the RULESURF command.

From the AutoCAD main menu select **1 "Begin a NEW drawing"**. Name the drawing anything you desire.

Draw the following polylines (size is not important) with the **PLINE** command in the World Coordinate System as shown (Fig. 5-4). Do **not** use the 3DPOLY command or the LINE command.

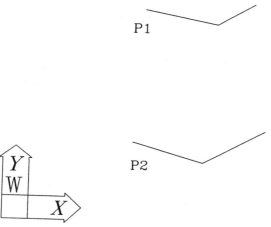

Figure 5-4 Defining curves for RULESURF.

Now enter the **RULESURF** command. From the root screen menu, select **3D**, then select **RULSURF**. The command format is:

❖ **Command:**RULESURF
Select first defining curve:
pick first line at **P1**
Select second defining curve:
pick second line at **P2**

The result should look like Fig. 5-5.

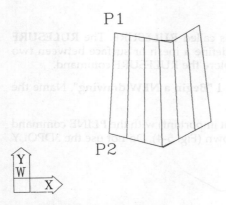

Figure 5-5 RULESURF command.

Now **UNDO** the 3DMESH created by RULESURF with the **U** command. Type U only one time to erase only the previous mesh. Now select the system variable **SURFTB1** from the screen menu.

Set the **SURFTAB1** variable equal to **15** as shown.

❖ **Command:**SURFTAB1
'SETVAR Variable name or ? <SURTAB1>: SURFTAB1
New value for SURFTAB1 <6>:
type **15 [ENTER]**

Now reenter the **RULESURF** command and select points **P1** and **P2** again as shown before (Fig. 5-6).

❖ **Command:**RULESURF
Select first defining curve:
pick first line at **P1**
Select second defining curve:
pick second line at **P2**

The lines in the mesh should now be closer together (Fig. 5-6).

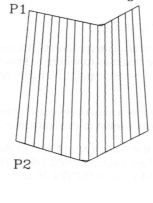

Figure 5-6 Setting the SURFTAB1 system variable.

Now **ERASE** only the mesh, leaving the two polylines and reenter the **RULESURF** command again. Select the points at **P1** and **P2** shown (Fig. 5-7) for the first and second defining curves.

❖ **Command:**RULESURF
Select first defining curve:
pick first line at **P1**
Select second defining curve:
pick second line at **P2**

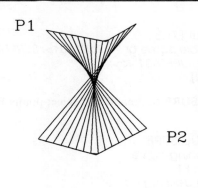

Figure 5-7 Variations with RULESURF.

Notice the difference in the mesh. The creation of the mesh is **"twisted"** around the two points. Care must be taken as to where to select the two points for the defining curves. In the above example point P1 was directly connected to point P2.

RULESURF allows you to create a mesh between any two entities. **RULESURF** will try to connect the vertices closest to the endpoints selected.

Now **erase** everything on the screen using the ERASE command with the **window** option. Draw the two circles shown below (Fig. 5-8) with the same center points. Select **3D** and then **SURFTB1** from the screen menu and set **SURFTAB1** equal to **25**.

❖ **Command:SURFTAB1**
  'SETVAR Variable name or ? <SURFTAB1>: SURFTAB1
  New value for SURFTAB1 <15>:
  type **25 [ENTER]**

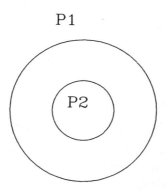

Figure 5-8 Defining curves for RULESURF.

Now enter the **RULESURF** command again and select the larger circle as the first defining curve P1 and the smaller circle as the second defining curve P2 (Fig. 5-9).

❖ **Command:**RULESURF
   Select first defining curve:
   pick first circle **P1**
   Select second defining curve:
   pick second circle **P2**

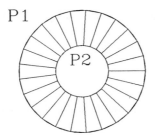

Figure 5-9 Circular surface mesh.

Notice that the **larger** the system variable SURFTAB1 is set, the more definition the mesh has.

You can use the DVIEW command to view the mesh from another angle. Enter the DVIEW command:

❖ **Command:DVIEW**
Select objects:
type **C** for crossing and place a window around both circles and press **[ENTER]**
Camera/TArget/Distance/POints/PAn
/Zoom/TWist/CLip/Hide/Off/Undo/<eXit>:
type **CAmera [ENTER]**
Enter angle from X-Y plane<90.00>:
type **35 [ENTER]**
Enter angle in X-Y plane from X axis<-90.00>:
type **35 [ENTER]**

Notice that the mesh is flat in the WCS where it was created (Fig. 5-10). Meshes can be created on any defined coordinate system.

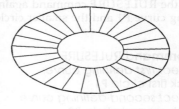

Figure 5-10 Changing your viewpoint with DVIEW.

Exit DVIEW by pressing **[ENTER]** and enter the **PLAN** command to return to the PLAN view.

❖ **Command:PLAN**
<Current UCS>/UCS/World:
press **[ENTER]**

Then enter the **ZOOM** command with the **A** (all) option to view the entire drawing limits.

❖ **Command:ZOOM**
All/Center/Dynamic/Extents/
Left/Prev/Window/<Scale(X)>:
type **A [ENTER]**

Now **erase** everything on the screen with the ERASE window option.

TABSURF COMMAND

The **TABSURF** command (tabulated surfaces) does not require two entities. It requires one entity as a path curve and then a direction vector. The mesh or surface is extruded from the path curve selected relative to a direction and distance of another selected entity on the drawing.

Draw the following objects (Fig. 5-11). Use the **PLINE** command to draw the polyline on the left and the **LINE** command to draw the line on the right.

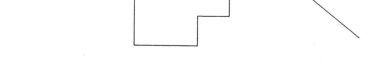

Figure 5-11 Path curve and direction vector.

Now enter the **TABSURF** command. Select **3D** from the root screen menu, then select **TABSURF**.

❖ **Command:**TABSURF
  Select Path curve:
  pick the polyline at left
  Select direction vector:
  pick the line

The polyline should have been changed to six **3DFACES** as shown in Fig. 5-12.

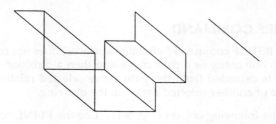

Figure 5-12 TABSURF command.

Undo the previous operation so that the original polyline and line appear as above (Fig. 5-11). Type **U**, then **[ENTER]**. Then use REDRAW to redisplay the polyline.

Now enter the **PEDIT** (polyline edit) command. Type PEDIT.

Select the polyline on the left as the polyline to edit. Then select the **Spline** curve option.

❖ **Command:**PEDIT
   Select polyline:
   select the polyline
   Close/Join/Width/Edit vertex/
   Fit curve/Spline curve/Decurve/
   Undo/eXit<X>:
   type **Spline [ENTER]**
   Then press **[ENTER]** to exit the PEDIT command.

The drawing should look as like (Fig. 5-13).

Figure 5-13 Changing the path curve.

Select the **Surftab1** system variable from the screen menu and set it to equal **20** as shown.

❖ **Command:**SURFTAB1
'SETVAR Variable name or ? <SURFTAB1>: SURFTAB1
New value for SURFTAB1<6> :
type **20 [ENTER]**

Now enter the **TABSURF** command again and select the new **Spline** curved **polyline** as the **path** curve and the **line** as the **direction** vector as we did before.

❖ **Command:**TABSURF
Select Path curve:
pick the polyline at left
Select direction vector:
pick the line

The drawing should look like Fig. 5-14.

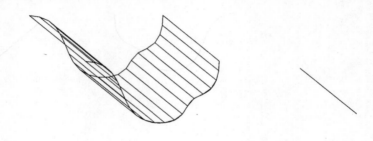

Figure 5-14 TABSURF command.

Now **erase** the 3D mesh and the polyline just created. Leave the line on the right on the screen. Now draw a circle with a small radius in its place as shown below (Fig. 5-15).

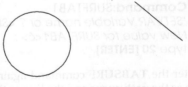

Figure 5-15 Path curve and direction vector.

Enter the TABSURF command again.

❖ **Command:**TABSURF
   Select Path curve:
   pick the circle
   Select direction vector:
   pick the line

The result is shown on the next page (Fig. 5-16).

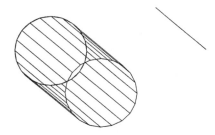

Figure 5-16 TABSURF command.

☞ **NOTE:** If you pick the line (direction vector) near the left endpoin
then the mesh will be drawn to the right. If you pick the line
near the right endpoint, the mesh will be drawn to the left.

Erase everything from the screen so we can create the next 3D mesh.

REVSURF COMMAND

The **REVSURF** command is a more complex command because it uses a "grid
type" mesh with both columns and rows. REVSURF means **surfaces of** revolution. With the REVSURF command a mesh or surface is revolved around a fixed
axis.

The system variables **SURFTAB1** and **SURFTAB2** are both used to control the
mesh created with the **REVSURF** command. Let's first set both **SURFTAB1**
and **SURFTAB2** to equal **20**.

Select the **3D** option from the root screen menu. Then select **Surftab2**.

❖ **Command:**SURFTAB2
'SETVAR Variable name or ? <SURFTAB2>; SURFTAB2
New value for SURFTAB2 <6>:
type **20 [ENTER]**

SURFTAB1 should also be set to equal **20**; if it is not, then change it as you did
above.

Now draw the line and polyline on the screen as shown (Fig. 5-17).

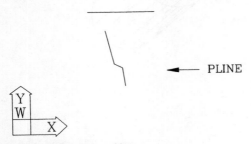

PLINE

Figure 5-17 Polyline and line.

Now enter the **PEDIT** (polyline edit) command. Select the polyline as the polyline to edit. Then select the **Fit curve** option.

> ❖ **Command:**PEDIT
> *Select polyline:*
> select the polyline, then press **[ENTER]**
> *Close/Join/Width/Edit vertex/*
> *Fit curve/Spline curve/Decurve*
> */Undo/eXIT<X>:*
> type **Fit [ENTER]**
> Exit the PEDIT command by pressing **[ENTER]** again.

The drawing should look like Fig. 5-18.

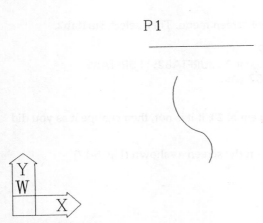

P1

Figure 5-18 PEDIT fit curve.

Now enter the **REVSURF** command. Select **3D** from the root screen menu, then select the **REVSURF** command.

❖ **Command:**REVSURF
   Select path curve:
   pick the polyline
   Select axis of revolution:
   pick the line at point **P1**
   Start angle <0>:
   press **[ENTER]**
   Included angle (+=ccw, -=cw)<Full circle>:
   press **[ENTER]**

The result is shown below (Fig. 5-19). You can specify the amount to revolve the object around the axis at the **"Include angle"** prompt. A value of **360** will produce a full revolution. The point you select on the **a**xis will determine how the object will be revolved around the axis.

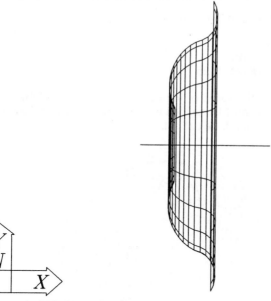

Figure 5-19 REVSURF command.

Now enter the **DVIEW** command. Type DVIEW.

❖ **Command:**DVIEW
   Select objects:
   type **C** for crossing, place a window around the entire object
   or any part of the object, and press **[ENTER]**
   *Camera/TArget/Distance/POints/PAn
   /Zoom/TWist/CLip/Hide/Off/Undo/<eXit>:*
   type **CAmera [ENTER]**
   Enter angle from X-Y plane <90.00>:
   type **35 [ENTER]**
   Enter angle in X-Y plane from X axis <90.00>:
   type **20 [ENTER]**

The object should look like the one below (Fig. 5-20). You can use the **DVIEW** Zoom option at this point to reduce the size of the drawing to fit it on your screen. Press **[ENTER]** again to exit the **DVIEW** command.

Use the **HIDE** command for hidden line removal.

❖ **Command:**HIDE
   Regenerating drawing.
   Removing hidden lines: 1125

☞ **NOTE:** Depending on the speed of your computer, a considerable amount of time may be needed to regenerate a mesh when using the HIDE command. Be patient.

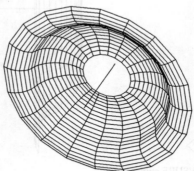

Figure 5-20 DVIEW and REVSURF.

Now exit the AutoCAD drawing editor using the END command. Type END.

❖ **Command:**END

EDGESURF COMMAND

The EDGESURF command is used to create a mesh between **four** known **edges, or sides. EDGESURF** means **edge-defined surface** patch and lets you draw a coons surface patch between four edges. You must have exactly four sides. Let's try the EDGESURF command now.

From the AutoCAD main menu select **1, Begin a NEW drawing.** Name the drawing "**MESH**".

Draw the shape below with the **LINE** and ARC commands. Use the ENDpoint object snap mode to make sure that all the corners are closed (Fig. 5-21).

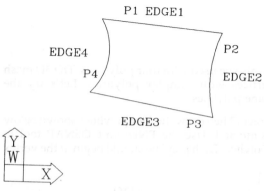

Figure 5-21 Four edges for EDGESURF command.

Before we create the mesh with the EDGESURF command, the system variables **SURFTAB1** and **SURFTAB2** should be set to **20** to control the density of the mesh. Select **3D** from the root screen menu. Now select **SURFTB1** and enter a value of **20**. Then select **SURFTB2** from the screen menu and enter a value of **20** also.

Now enter the **EDGESURF** command. Select the **EDGESURF** command from the screen menu.

❖ **Command:**EDGESURF
Select edge 1:
pick at **P1**
Select edge 2:
pick at **P2**
Select edge 3:
pick at **P3**
Select edge 4:
pick at **P4**

Make sure to pick all points at the specified locations shown.

The mesh is created between the four lines as shown in Fig. 5-22.

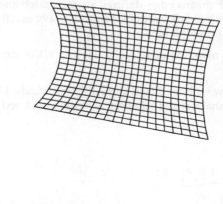

Figure 5-22 EDGESURF command.

The **EDGESURF** command can also be used with four **polylines**. The 3D mesh will find the appropriate vertices with complex polylines. Let's try the EDGESURF command with some polylines.

First erase everything on the screen. Then draw the four polylines shown below (Fig. 5-23) with the PLINE command. Use the **ENDpoint OSNAP** tool to connect the endpoints of each polyline. Each polyline should begin at the vertex points indicated.

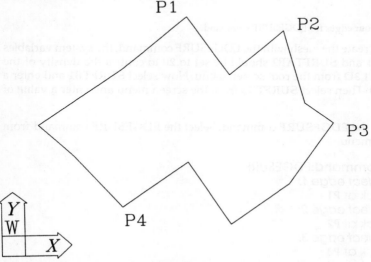

Figure 5-23 Four polylines for EDGESURF command.

☞ **NOTE:** There must be four separate connected polylines.

Now enter the **PEDIT** command and use the **Fit curve** option to smooth out the first polyline. Type PEDIT.

❖ **Command:**PEDIT
Select polyline:
select the first polyline at **P1**, then **[ENTER]** (Fig. 5-23)
Close/Join/Width/Edit vertex/
Fit curve/Spline curve/Decurve
/Undo/eXit<X>:
type **Fit [ENTER]**
Close/Join/Width/Edit vertex/
Fit curve/Spline curve/Decurve
/Undo/eXit<X>:
type **X [ENTER]**

After exiting the PEDIT command, you must reenter the PEDIT command to perform a fit curve on each of the other polylines. The result should now similar to the drawing below (Fig. 5-24).

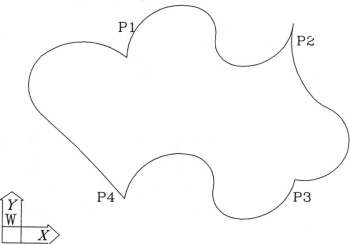

Figure 5-24 Four fit curve polylines.

Now enter the **EDGESURF** command. Select 3D from the root screen menu, then select **EDGESURF**. Pick near the points P1, P2, P3, and P4 shown in Fig. 5-24 above for each edge (pick near the beginning of each polyline).

❖ **Command:**EDGESURF
Select edge 1:
pick at **P1**
Select edge 2:
pick at **P2**
Select edge 3:
pick at **P3**
Select edge 4:
pick at **P4**

The result should look similar to the illustration shown (Fig. 5-25).

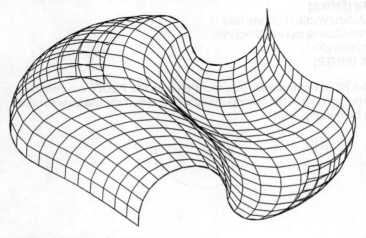

Figure 5-25 EDGESURF command.

The system variables **SURFTAB1** and **SURFTAB2** should be set large enough to give the appropriate density to form the shape desired. You must also be careful as to where you select each polyline within the EDGESURF command. Try to pick them near the same end points on each polyline.

Now exit the AutoCAD drawing editor. Use the END command. Type **END** the command prompt line.

❖ **Command:**END

3DMESH COMMAND

The **3DMESH** command is used to create general polygon meshes which cannot be otherwise created with **RULESURF, TABSURF, REVSURF,** and **EDGESURF.** Normally, you will not need to use this command. The **3DMESH** command can be used to create **custom 3D meshes,** where you define the density and location of each vertex in the mesh. Creating a 3D mesh with this command is much more time consuming than with the others, so if a mesh can be created with the other 3D commands, use them instead.

The **3DMESH** command needs a defined "matrix" (cross-grid) size. You are prompted for the **M** and **N** size of the matrix where **M** is the number of vertices in one direction and **N** is the number of vertices in the other direction (Fig. 5-26).

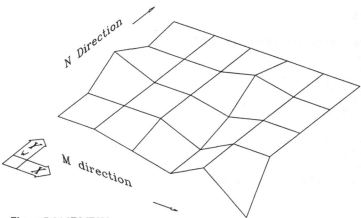

Figure 5-26 3DMESH.

Try the **3DMESH** command. From the AutoCAD **main menu** select **1, Begin a NEW drawing.** Name the drawing "3DMESH".

From within the AutoCAD drawing editor select the **3D** option from the screen menu. Turn the **GRID ON [F7]** and **SNAP ON [F9].** Now select the 3DMESH command and look at Fig. 5-27. AutoCAD will now prompt you for the Mesh M size. Answer the prompts with the following responses.

❖ **Command:**3DMESH
Mesh M size:
enter **6 [ENTER]**
Mesh N size:
enter **5 [ENTER]**
Vertex (0,0):
pick **P1** (Fig. 5-27)
Vertex (0,1):
pick **P2**
Vertex (0,2):
pick **P3**
Vertex (0,3):
pick **P4**
Vertex (0,4):
pick **P5**
Vertex (1,0):
pick **P6** (second column, Fig. 5-27)
Vertex (1,1):
pick **P7**
Vertex (1,2):
pick **P8**
Vertex (1,3):
pick **P9**
Vertex (1,4):
pick **P10**
Vertex (2,0):
pick **P11** (third column, Fig. 5-27)
.
.
.
Vertex (5,4):
pick **P30**

You must pick all 30 points as shown. After picking the last point (P30), the mesh should appear similar to the one on the next page (Fig. 5-27):

P5	P10	P15	P20	P25	P30
P4	P9	P14	P19	P24	P29
P3	P8	P13	P18	P23	P28
P2	P7	P12	P17	P22	P27
P1	P6	P11	P16	P21	P26

Figure 5-27 Picking points for a mesh.

Now enter the **DVIEW** command to view the mesh from an another angle.

❖ **Command:**DVIEW
Select objects:
type **C** for crossing, place a window around the entire object, and press **[ENTER]**
Camera/TArget/Distance/POints/PAn
/Zoom/TWist/CLip/Hide/Off/Undo/<eXit>:
type **CAmera [ENTER]**
Enter angle from X-Y plane<90.00>:
type **35 [ENTER]**
Enter angle in X-Y plane from X axis<-90.00>:
type **35 [ENTER]**

The mesh should now look like the one below (Fig. 5-28).

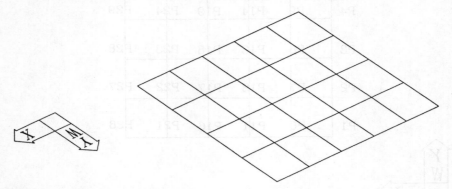

Figure 5-28 3DMESH command.

Now press **[ENTER]** to **exit** the DVIEW command. Turn SNAP OFF **[F9]**.

EDITING A 3D MESH

Edit the mesh with the **PEDIT** command. Enter the **PEDIT** command and select the mesh (anywhere on the mesh) as the polyline to edit.

❖ **Command:**PEDIT
  Select polyline:
  select the mesh, then **[ENTER]**
  Edit vertex/Smooth surface/
  Desmooth/Mclose/Nclose
  /Undo/eXit<X>:
  type **E** for edit vertex, then **[ENTER]**

Notice that an **X** will appear at one of the vertices (at the first point P1 of the mesh) shown in Fig. 5-29.

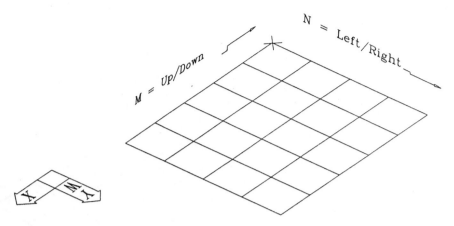

Figure 5-29 Editing a mesh with PEDIT.

The **X** can be moved with the **Next, Previous, Left, Right, Up** or **Down** options
to any vertex you wish to edit when the next prompt appears:

Vertex (0,0). Next/Previous/Left/Right/
Up/Down/Move/Regen/eXit <N>:
press **M** for move **[ENTER]**
Enter New location:
type **.XY**
of
type **INT [ENTER]**
of
pick **P1** or the X
need z:
type **1.25 [ENTER]**

The mesh looks like Fig. 5-30.

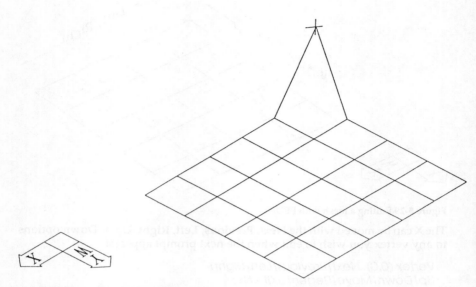

Figure 5-30 Editing a Mesh With PEDIT.

Now move the **X** over with **Next, Previous, Up, or Down** options within the **PEDIT** command and change the mesh to look similar to the one shown in Fig. 5-31. The illustration shows the directions for the up, down, left and right positioning of the "**X**" with the PEDIT command. If you simply press the **[ENTER]** key continuously, the "**X**" will move to the **next** vertex in the mesh. If you type **P (previous)** and **[ENTER]**, the "**X**" will move back to the last vertex. If you type **U** and **[ENTER]**, the "**X**" will move **up** in the mesh. If you type **D** and **[ENTER]**, the "**X**" will move **down** in the mesh. Use the "**M**" **(move)** option to move the vertex in the **Z** direction after positioning it at the desired vertex in the mesh. Then use the pointing device to **pick** the new locations of the vertices in the **Z** axis. Yours may not look exactly the same as the one shown in Fig. 5-31.

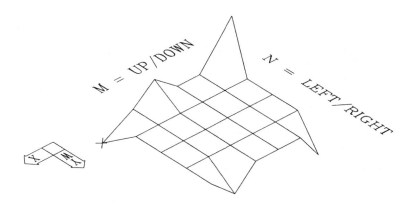

Figure 5-31 Final 3DMESH.

Exit the PEDIT command by pressing the [Ctrl] and [C] keys together and use the HIDE command for hidden line removal. Type HIDE.

❖ **Command:**HIDE
   Regenerating drawing.
   Removing hidden lines: 125

Use the **ZOOM** command from the keyboard and type in a ZOOM factor of .5x to reduce your view of the mesh.

❖ **Command:**ZOOM
   All/Center/Dynamic/Extents/
   Left/Prev/Window/<Scale(X)>:
   type **.5x [ENTER]**

Copy the mesh with the **COPY** command three times and place the copies on the screen as shown in Fig. 5-32. Use the **Multiple** option within the **COPY** command.

❖ **Command:**COPY
Select objects:
select mesh
select objects:
press **[ENTER]**
<Base point or displacement>Multiple:
type **M [ENTER]**
Base point:
pick a point to copy from
<Second point of displacement:
pick a point to copy to
<Second point of displacement:
pick three locations to copy to (Fig. 5-32)

press **[ENTER]** to exit the COPY command or use **[Ctrl]** and **[C]** to cancel.

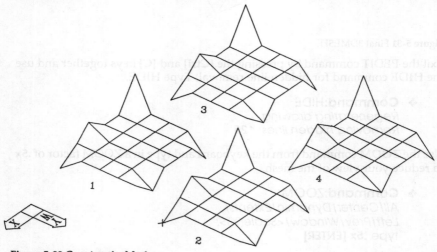

Figure 5-32 Copying the Mesh.

CUBIC MESH

The meshes can be converted to create different types of meshes. Try a CUBIC mesh.

From the AutoCAD root screen menu select **EDIT**. Then select **PEDIT** and select mesh 2 as the polyline to edit and use the "Smooth" option to smooth out the mesh.

❖ **Command:**PEDIT
Select objects:
select **mesh 2**, then **[ENTER]**
Edit vertex/Smooth surface/
Desmooth/Mclose/Nclose
/Undo/eXit<X>:
type **S [ENTER]**

The mesh should look like Fig. 5-33. This is a CUBIC mesh.

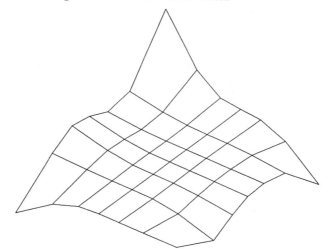

Figure 5-33 Cubic mesh.

QUADRATIC MESH

Now let's change this to a QUADRATIC mesh.

Exit the **PEDIT** command by pressing **[ENTER]**. Then reenter the **PEDIT** command through the screen menus and select mesh 3 as the polyline to edit.

> ❖ **Command:**PEDIT
> *Select objects:*
> select mesh 3, then **[ENTER]**

From the screen menu select the **PolyVars** option and a dialogue box will appear. From the dialogue box select the **Quadratic** option at the top left of the dialogue box. Then select the **Smooth** option again.

> *Edit vertex/Smooth surface/*
> *Desmooth/Mclose/Nclose*
> */Undo/eXit<X>:*
> type **S [ENTER]**

The mesh now looks like the one below (Fig. 5-34). This is a QUADRATIC mesh. This is slightly different from the CUBIC mesh.

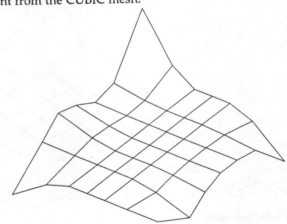

Figure 5-34 Quadratic mesh.

BEZIER MESH

Now change mesh 4 to a BEZIER mesh.

Exit the **PEDIT** command by pressing **[ENTER]** again. Then reenter the **PEDIT** command through the screen menu again and select mesh 4 as the polyline to edit.

❖ **Command:**PEDIT
   Select objects:
   select mesh 4, then **[ENTER]**

Select the **Poly**Vars option from the screen menu again and select the **Bezier** option from the dialogue box at the lower left. Then use the **Smooth** option from the **PEDIT** command again.

Edit vertex/Smooth surface/
Desmooth/Mclose/Nclose
/Undo/eXit<X>:
type **S [ENTER]**

Mesh 4 now looks like the one below (Fig. 5-35). This is a BEZIER mesh.

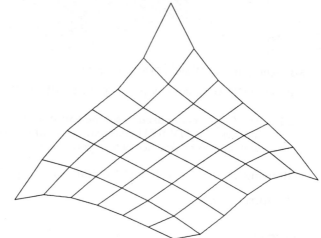

Figure 5-35 Bezier mesh.

☞ **NOTE:** Do not exit the PEDIT command until instructed to do so.

Select the **UDensity** option from the screen menu and set it to **20**. Then select the **VDensity** option and set it to **20** also. These options set the **SURFU** and **SURFV** system variables and will change the size of the spacing of the grids in the mesh. From the **PEDIT** command line select the **Smooth** option again.

Be patient. The mesh may take some time to regenerate.

Figure 5-36 shows the differences in the types of meshes that can be generated with the 3DMESH command by setting the **Udensity** and **Vdensity** options. Exit the PEDIT command by pressing **[ENTER]**.

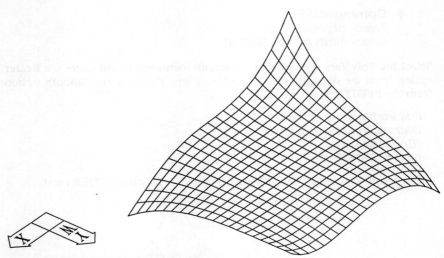

Figure 5-36 Setting UDENSITY and VDENSITY variables.

Now exit the PEDIT command by pressing the **[Ctrl]** and **[C]** keys together.

☞ **NOTE:** The **Polyvars** are used to **set** the **variables** for the display of the meshes. The **3DMESH** command is a difficult command and it will take some practice before you master it.

Exit the drawing editor now with the END command. Type **END**.

❖ **Command:**END

3D OBJECTS

AutoCAD Release 10 has some built in 3D objects. They can be accessed from the **DRAW** pull-down window under **3D Construction....**

Or you can access them from the screen menus by selecting the **3D OBJECTS** option after selecting **3D** from the root screen menu.

From the AutoCAD **main menu** select **1, Begin a NEW drawing**. Name the drawing **"SPHERE"**.

Select **Draw** from the pull-down windows. Then select **3D Construction....** A dialogue box appears. All of the previously discussed AutoCAD 3D commands can be accessed from this dialogue box.

The 3D objects can be selected to create any size shape. Let's try one of them from the **3D OBJECTS** dialogue box. Select the **SPHERE** option box in the upper right corner with the pointing device.

AutoCAD prompts:

Please wait... Loading 3D Objects.
Center of sphere:
pick a point near the center of the screen.
Diameter/<radius>:
type **3 [ENTER]**
Number of longitudinal segments <16>:
press **[ENTER]**
Number of latitudinal segments <16>:
press **[ENTER]**

This creates the sphere in the PLAN view of the World Coordinate System (WCS). You will need to use the **DVIEW** command with the **CAMERA** option to view the sphere. You can use angles of 35 to produce the sphere in Fig. 5-37. Type **DVIEW.**

❖ **Command:**DVIEW
  Select objects:
  type **C** for crossing and place a window around the entire object, then press **[ENTER]**
  Camera/TArget/Distance/POints/PAn
  /Zoom/TWist/CLip/Hide/Off/Undo/<eXit>:
  type **CAmera [ENTER]**
  Enter angle from X-Y plane<90.00>:
  type **35 [ENTER]**
  Enter angle in X-Y plane from X axis<-90.00>:
  type **35 [ENTER]**
  press **[ENTER]** again to exit the DVIEW command.

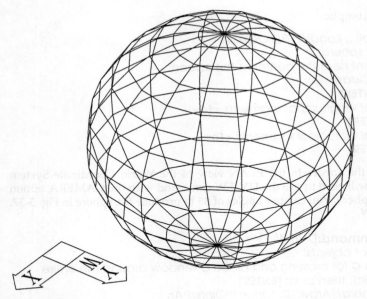

Figure 5-37 3D sphere.

3D SYSTEM VARIABLES

As discussed earlier, the spacing between the lines in a mesh is determined by the AutoCAD system variables called **SURFTAB1** and **SURFTAB2**. (These variables change the distance between columns and rows in a mesh.)

Below is a summary of the functions of SURFTAB1 and SURFTAB2.

SURFTAB1

SURFTAB1 controls the **density** of a mesh created with **RULESURF** and **TABSURF**. These are not actually cross-grids but single lines forming the mesh dependent on the points picked. **SURFTAB1** controls the **density of single line meshes.**

SURFTAB2

SURFTAB2 is used in conjunction with **SURFTAB1** to form all **cross-grid meshes.** SURFTAB2 sets the spacing for either the horizontal or vertical lines in the mesh depending on the points picked to create the mesh.

SURFTAB2 and SURFTAB1 together control the **density** of any **cross-grid mesh** as created with the **REVSURF** and **EDGESURF** commands. These system variables can be accessed by selecting the **3D** option from the root screen menu.

They can be changed at any time and only control the density of the 3D meshes. The more dense the mesh, the slower the REDRAW or REGEN time for the drawing.

Polygon meshes can be open or closed and are used preferably when you need to draw an object as one entity.

SETVAR COMMAND

The SETVAR command can also be used to change these system variables. To use the **SETVAR** command, type SETVAR.

❖ **Command:**SETVAR
Variable name or ?:
type **SURFTAB1** or **SURFTAB2 [ENTER]**
New value for SURFTAB1<6> :
enter a value, then press **[ENTER]**

Now exit the drawing editor again with the END command. Type END.

❖ **Command:**END

☞ NOTE: The **SURFTAB1** and **SURFTAB2** system variables must be set to a desired density before a mesh is created with any of the 3D mesh commands to determine its density.

SUMMARY

You now have all the tools necessary to effectively design 3D models with AutoCAD. Initially you may find some of the procedures cumbersome to work with, but with practice you will become proficient.

Chapter 6 will discuss how to add text and dimensions to your drawing. Also, editing 3D meshes and system errors that you may encounter will be discussed.

3D NOTES

ADDING TEXT TO 3D DRAWINGS

A dding text to a 3D drawing is done the same way as in a 2D drawing. You must, however, be aware of the UCS you are currently working in when placing text. Like any other entity, text will be drawn in the same orientation as the current UCS icon indicates.

Text can be added on any plane, any defined UCS, or can be placed parallel to your view (aligned with the screen). Both the DTEXT and TEXT commands can be used to place text strings.

To place lines of text on a particular plane or UCS, you must first change to the UCS, with the UCS command. Then place the text with the DTEXT or TEXT command as usual. Text should be placed after the drawing is completed and rotated to the desired viewpoint. Let's try placing text on a 3D model.

From the AutoCAD main menu, select 2 "Edit an EXISTING drawing".

Call up the drawing called "MODEL" which you created in Chap. 2.

Make sure the drawing looks like the one here (Fig. 6-1). Use the VPOINT or DVIEW commands to rotate the model into a similar position if necessary.

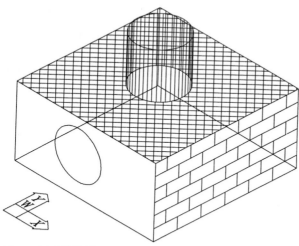

Figure 6-1 "MODEL" drawing.

Now use the **UCS** command with the **View** option to set the UCS parallel to the screen. Type UCS.

❖ **Command:**UCS
Origin/Zaxis/3point/Entity/View/
X/Y/Z/Prev/Restore/Save/Del/?/<World>:
type **View [ENTER]**

This will cause the UCS icon to appear in the lower left corner of the screen with the X-Y plane parallel to the screen or your viewing direction, as shown below (Fig. 6-2). It does not matter how the object is orientated. Now all entities drawn while working in this UCS will be parallel to the screen. This is the most effective way to label 3D models, with all the text on one plane.

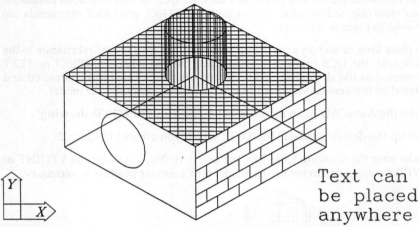

Text can
be placed
anywhere

Figure 6-2 UCS view option.

Add the text with the **DTEXT** command (Fig. 6-2) at about the same location shown. Enter the DTEXT command.

❖ **Command:**DTEXT
Start point or Align/
Center/Fit/Middle/Right/Style:
pick start point (Fig. 6-2)
Height <0.20>:
press **[ENTER]**
Rotation angle <0.00>:
press **[ENTER]**
Text:
type a line of text,then **[ENTER]**
Text:

Continue to type text lines, and then press **[ENTER]** when each is complete.

Type the three lines of text shown (Fig. 6-2).

The text we just placed using the **UCS** command with the **View** option should be used after the drawing is completed and rotated at the desired angle needed for the plot. It can be used at anytime, but once the **text** is placed parallel to the screen and the drawing is rotated to another viewpoint, the text may disappear or become distorted.

A good idea is to place all the text on a separate layer so that layer can be **frozen** before changing your viewpoint of the drawing.

Now restore the UCS called **FRONT** with the UCS dialogue box. Select **SET-TINGS** from the pull-down windows. Then select **UCS dialogue.** Make the FRONT UCS active by placing a checkmark in the box to the left of the UCS named **FRONT** under "**current**". Then pick **OK** at the bottom of the dialogue box.

Use the ERASE command and erase the circle in the FRONT view. Now use the **TEXT** command to place a line of text on the front view of the drawing as shown (Fig. 6-3).

❖ **Command:**TEXT
 Start point or Align/
 Center/Fit/Middle/Right/Style:
 pick start point
 Rotation angle<0.00>:
 press **[ENTER]**
 Text:
 type a line of text, then **[ENTER]**

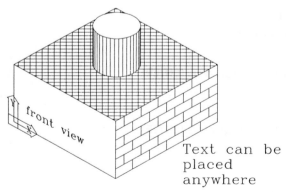

Text can be placed anywhere

Figure 6-3 Adding TEXT to the drawing.

You may also align the text with a selected entity on the drawing. The **UCS** command with the **Entity** option can be selected to do so.

Exit the drawing editor and save the drawing called "**MODEL**" with the END command.

Type **END** to save this drawing and return to the AutoCAD main menu.

❖ **Command:**END

☞   **NOTE:** If the HIDE command is used after the text is placed it will not
hide the text with a 3D drawing. Therefore you should place text
on a separate layer so you can **freeze** the layer and hide the text.

USING X-Y-Z FILTERS

The AutoCAD filters can be used just as they are used on any 2D drawing. The
only difference is that you now have a **Z axis** filter which can be used. The X-Y-Z
filters can be used whenever AutoCAD prompts you for a point, such as with:

"From point:"

The AutoCAD filters are especially useful for extracting points from existing
entities of an object. Let's use the filters to draw a circle in the center of the front
view or "front UCS" of the 3D model we created in Chap. 4 (Fig. 6-4).

From the AutoCAD main menu, select **2 "Edit an EXISTING drawing"**. Load
the drawing called **"UCS"**. Orientate the drawing with the DVIEW or VPOINT
command so it looks like the one in Fig. 6-4.

First make the **UCS** labeled **"FRONT"** the current UCS. Select **SETTINGS** from
the pull-down windows. Next select **UCS Dialogue**. Move the checkmark
under **current** next to the UCS called FRONT and pick **OK** from the bottom of
the dialogue box.

Now, enter the **CIRCLE** command and select the **CEN,RAD** option.

❖ **Command:**CIRCLE
3P/2P/TTR/<Center point>:
type **.X [ENTER]**
of
type **MID** for MIDpoint object snap **[ENTER]**
MIDpoint of
pick line **AB**
of (Need YZ)
type **MID** for MIDpoint object snap **[ENTER]**
pick line **BC**
Diameter/<Radius>:
type **1.25 [ENTER]**

The drawing should look like Fig. 6-4.

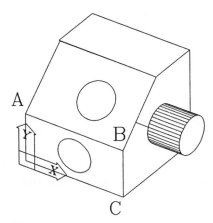

Figure 6-4 Using AutoCAD X-Y-Z filters.

The circle should be exactly in the center of the front face of the model. The
center point location of the circle was extracted or filtered from the **MID**points
of the horizontal and vertical lines in the **FRONT UCS**. Remember that the X
and Y axes directions and the UCS origin have been changed in this UCS and
all filtering is done with reference to the current UCS and its origin location.

Do not quit this drawing yet. We will dimension this drawing in the next
section.

☞ **NOTE:** You may get strange results when trying to select entities to
filter points from if they reside on a UCS other than the
current UCS.

DIMENSIONING IN 3D

Placing dimensions on a 3D model can be somewhat confusing at first. You
should apply the same rules as placing text. First, be aware of the current UCS
you are working in.

Secondly, all dimensions should be placed on the drawing using the **object
snaps** (OSNAPS) to ensure precision. The **object snaps** will override all UCSs
and snap to a specified location of an existing entity no matter what UCS it is
on.

Do not attempt to dimension without using the **OSNAPS**.

You should not attempt to place dimensions when working in the **View** option
within the **UCS** command. Dimensions can be placed on any other UCS and
will be displayed at the same X-Y axes orientation as that **UCS**. If you are going
to create a new UCS to dimension in, you should use either the **UCS entity** or
3Point options.

Dimension a 3D model only after it has been completed and rotated to the desired position needed to plot. When you change your viewpoint of the drawing after the dimensions are placed, the dimensions may disappear or become distorted. Dimensions and text placed on one UCS may not look the same after changing your viewpoint.

Dimension the model in Fig. 6-5. Make the **UCS** labeled "**FRONT**" current. Select **SETTINGS** from the pull-down windows, then select **UCS dialogue box**. The **FRONT** UCS should be set current already. Now dimension the bottom line in the FRONT view.

First make sure the dimension text height is set properly. To do so change the DIMSCALE dimension variable. From the command prompt line type SETVAR (set variable).

❖ **Command:**SETVAR
   Variable name or ?:
   type **DIMSCALE [ENTER]**
   New value for DIMSCALE <1.0000>:
   type **6 [ENTER]**

Now enter the **DIMENSION** command. Select **DIM** from the root screen menu.

❖ **Command:**DIM
   Dim:
   select **LINEAR**
   select **HORIZ [ENTER]**
   First extension line origin or [ENTER] to select:
   type **END** for ENDpoint object snap **[ENTER]**
   of
   pick **P1**
   Second extension line origin:
   type **END** for ENDpoint object snap **[ENTER]**
   of
   pick **P2**
   Dimension line location:
   pick **below the line**
   Dimension Text<1.000>:
   press **[ENTER]**

Press the **[Ctrl]** key and the **[C]** key together to exit the DIM command.

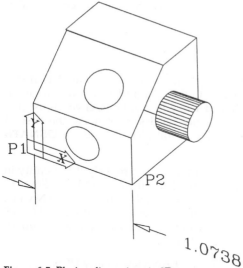

Figure 6-5 Placing dimensions in 3D.

Notice how the dimension was placed parallel to the current UCS (Fig. 6-5). All of the dimensions placed will be parallel to this UCS until you change to another UCS. To dimension the side of the model you will need to change to the UCS which is parallel to that side or you can **define** another **UCS** with the **UCS Entity** or **UCS 3Point** options.

Dimensions can also be placed in the World Coordinate System (**WCS**). And they will be parallel to the WCS, which would cause them to appear on the X-Y plane. This is probably the best plane to place most of the dimensions.

You will **not** be **allowed** to **dimension** with **perspective mode ON**. If you have perspective mode ON, turn it OFF before dimensioning. Place dimensions on a separate layer so they can be frozen when changing your viewpoint with DVIEW or VPOINT. Its a good idea also to save the completed dimensioned drawing as a view with the VIEW command so it can be restored at a later time. Perspective views with dimensions can also be saved with the VIEW command.

The best way to dimension a 3D drawing is to define a new UCS using the **UCS 3Point** option in conjunction with the **OSNAPS** so that you can have complete control over the placement of the dimensions.

If you would like to see the dimensioned model in perspective, you can do so by selecting the **Distance** option within the **DVIEW** command after the dimensions have been placed. Remember, dimensioning, drawing, and editing while **perspective** is turned **ON** are not permitted.

After you have completed the dimensions, if you are not sure that the dimension value displayed is correct, use the **DIST** (distance), command in the **WCS** to determine the actual value using the entities two endpoints. Then **explode** the dimension, erase the dimension text, and place the new dimension value in with the TEXT command.

EDITING 3D MODELS

The AutoCAD editing commands may react unusually with 3D models. If you try to edit an entity and it is not parallel to the current UCS, you will get an error message or a peculiar result. In order to **edit** a 3D model you must first change to the current UCS where the entity resides, then make the desired changes. Still you may not get the desired results. Try to use the **OSNAPS** whenever possible to do all editing.

Some of the EDIT commands will not seem to work properly if the entity in question has an extrusion which is perpendicular to the current UCS. Some of the EDIT commands will produce strange results unless you are in PLAN view. A good way to edit may be to set up three or four viewports with the VPORTS command and place the PLAN view of each of the UCSs in a separate viewport. Then you can edit all entities in their PLAN view.

All **edits** can be done more successfully in a **PLAN** view of any UCS.

CHPROP OR PROPERTIES

The **CHPROP** (change properties) command has been added to help with editing entities and can be used to change only the properties of an entity such as **color, linetype, layer, or thickness.** Using the **CHPROP** command is a more effective way to change a 3D entity.

To access the **CHPROP** command select the **MODIFY** pull-down window option, then select **Properties.** You can also access the **CHPROP** command by typing it at the command prompt line. Type **CHPROP**, then select the objects to change as usual.

ERROR MESSAGES

There are some 3D error messages that will appear at the command prompt line occasionally when you are editing or drawing. They are listed here.

"Entity not parallel with UCS"

You will get this message while you are trying to edit an entity which resides on a UCS other than the current UCS or when the entity extrudes perpendicular to the current UCS. This entity can be edited by changing to the UCS which is parallel to the entity's extrusion or by defining another UCS with the **UCS Entity** option. The **UCS Entity** option will allow you to create a new UCS parallel to the entity's extrusion, allowing you to edit it.

"4 not parallel with UCS"

If you use the CHANGE command and select several objects, this error message tells you how many of the selected entities will not be affected by CHANGE because they are not parallel to the current UCS.

"Pointing in PERSPECTIVE view not allowed here"

You will get this message if you try to draw or edit a drawing while **perspective** mode is ON. You should use the VIEW command to save the perspective view first, then turn **perspective** mode OFF, make any edits to the drawing, and restore the VIEW. The drawing will be displayed in the same perspective as it was saved with the VIEW command with all the edits made. You can also use multiple viewports to do the same thing. Set the model up in one viewport with **perspective ON** and in another with **perspective OFF**. Make all edits in the viewport with **perspective** turned **OFF**.

"3D Polygon mesh entity does not define a coordinate system"

This message will appear if you try to define a new User Coordinate System with the UCS commands **Entity** option while trying to align the new UCS with 3D mesh. A 3D mesh cannot be used as an entity to align a UCS to.

"Entities not parallel with UCS were ignored"

This message may appear while you are trying to edit a set of entities with the window option. Any entities inside the selected window that do not reside on the current UCS while editing will be ignored.

"View is not plan to UCS. Command results may not be obvious"

This message will appear while you are trying to edit or draw when the display of the drawing is not a PLAN view of the current UCS.

"Cannot find UCS Name"

This message will appear when you are trying to restore a UCS that has not been previously saved with the UCS command. You should check to see if the UCS name has been saved or check the spelling. Use the UCS dialogue box to check the names of all the User Coordinate Systems.

POINT SPECIFICATION WITH UCS

Each of the coordinate systems, whether it is a User Coordinate System (UCS) or the World Coordinate System (WCS), will have separate distinct origins and X, Y, and Z axes directions. All entities drawn on a particular UCS are always referenced from that UCSs origin location.

Points and entities can be drawn and specified with coordinates typed from the keyboard using absolute, relative, or polar coordinate input relative to the current UCS origin and axis directions.

When entering points from the keyboard using absolute, relative, or polar coordinate input, the Z value can be added after the X and Y values in the form (X,Y,Z). 0.00 is the default if a Z value is not typed in. Remember, when using any of the above means of inputting entities, make sure to mentally reference everything from the current UCS origin. For example, if you were to enter points such as @5,0 (relative mode), the points would be referenced from the last point picked with reference to the X and Y axis direction of the current UCS. If you need to reference a coordinate from the WCS rather than the current UCS, you can place an * in front of the coordinate values. For example, the coordinate input of *3,2,2 will specify a point relative to the origin of the WCS no matter what coordinate system is currently active.

COMMAND CHANGES

Most of the changes that appear in AutoCAD Release 10 have to do with the 3D commands. The major additions to AutoCAD are the UCS and VPORTS commands. Some of the editing commands react somewhat differently with 3D entities than with 2D entities. The following lists and explains some of the changes that have occurred within AutoCAD Release 10.

- The UCS command has been added to create separate planes or User Coordinate Systems to work in.

- The VPORTS command was added to enhance your display of the drawing by allowing you to work in up to four separate viewports.

- The DVIEW command has been added to allow for more options to orientate the display of a 3D model.

- The VPOINT 3D command has been added to the pull-down windows to provide an easy access to rotating your viewpoint.

- The PLAN command will return you to the PLAN view of the current UCS unless you specify otherwise.

- The REDRAWALL and REGENALL commands have been added to redraw and regenerate all viewports displayed. REGEN and REDRAW will only work within the active viewport.

- The 3DLINE command has been removed and replaced by the LINE command. The LINE command will now accept 3D coordinates.

- The PLINE command should not be used to draw from one plane to another. The 3DPOLY command is used to draw 3D polylines from one plane to another.

- 3D commands to generate simple to complex 3D shapes and 3D polygon meshes include 3DMESH, RULESURF, TABSURF, REVSURF, and EDGESURF.

- All entities now have X, Y, and Z coordinates in the drawing database.

- All entities and coordinates are always relative to the current UCS.

- **AXIS** tick marks cannot be used with multiple viewports.

- If the current UCS and the WCS are equal, the **GRID** command will display the entire drawing limits, if not, the grid will cover the entire screen or viewport.

- The **OSNAPS** do not pay attention to the current UCS but will snap to a geometric location of any given entity on any UCS. Therefore you are able to draw from a specific point on an existing entity in one UCS to a point on another entity which exists on a different UCS.

- Dimensions may react strangely when you are dimensioning from one UCS to another. Make sure to use **object snaps** when placing all dimensions.

- The RENAME command lets you rename blocks, layers, linetypes, text styles, views, viewport configurations, and UCSs.

- The STATUS command now also displays information on the current UCS.

- The PEDIT command can be used to edit regular 2D polylines, 3D polylines, and 3D meshes.

- Solid FILL can only be used in the current UCS PLAN view.

3D RULES

The following rules should be considered when developing 3D models with AutoCAD.

1. Be aware of what **UCS** is **current**. You can only draw in one UCS at a time.

2. **Save** each **UCS** created with a appropriate **name** so it can be restored as often as needed. Also **save** a **view** right after saving the UCS with the **VIEW** command with the same name. Then you will be able to restore a defined UCS and the view that you saved it at.

3. Use the **UCS 3Point** option when creating new User Coordinate Systems as much as possible. This is the most accurate way to define a UCS.

4. Use the AutoCAD **OSNAPS** when **drawing** or **editing** 3D models to snap to geometric locations of all entities whenever possible. Make sure to distinguish between geometric locations when using the OSNAPS. For example, when using the OSNAP ENDpoint tool, place the pick box near the end of the exact line desired and not near any other lines or objects so as not to confuse AutoCAD.

5. Begin drawing a 3D model by drawing the **outline** of the model as a **cube** showing the overall **length, width,** and **height** of the object on a **separate layer** with one color. Then build the model inside the cube on another layer with a different color. This will give you some boundaries to work inside. Then **freeze** the layer with the cube on it when the model is completed.

6. Try to **separate parts** of a model using **layers** as much as possible. As drawings get too crowded, it becomes almost impossible to understand what is going on with the drawing. You can alleviate this problem by **freezing layers** and eliminating parts of the drawing to make things a little clearer.

7. Use **FREEZE** and **THAW** in place of ON and OFF, especially when using the **HIDE** command to remove hidden lines. When using the HIDE command with a layer turned OFF, the lines of that layer will be invisible but things behind them may show up hidden anyway. This will give some very strange results. Also, more processing time is consumed when turning layers OFF rather than freezing them.

8. Place **text** on a separate **layer** so it can be frozen off of the drawing.

9. Use the **HIDE command sparingly.** The HIDE command is extremely time consuming on a complex 3D model. If you need to remove hidden lines from a drawing, it is not necessary to do so with the whole drawing. You can select parts of the drawing with the DVIEW command, then use the HIDE command.

10. Use the **VPORTS** command to separate your viewpoints, or **UCSs,** of the model.

11. Set up a **separate viewport** for each **UCS.** Try to **draw** in **PLAN view** in each UCS.

12. Use the **VPORTS** command to display **several viewports** on the screen at once. Set one viewport to display the isometric or pictorial view of a model. Set the other viewports to display the PLAN view of each UCS. Try to **draw** in the **viewports** that display the **PLAN** views. Once you get the viewports set up the way you want, **save** the **viewport configuration** with the **VPORTS** command **Save** option.

13. Keep **SNAP OFF** when using the **DVIEW** command. The horizontal and vertical scroll bars cannot be controlled with SNAP ON.

14. When using the DVIEW command, you do not need to select the objects to view. If you press [ENTER] for the prompt "Select objects:", you will get the AutoCAD house drawing. After you position the house as desired and exit the DVIEW command, your drawing will be rotated the same way.

15. Select **only** the **objects required** (by picking them or using a window) to view when using the DVIEW command. You do not need to select the entire drawing when orientating your display with the DVIEW command. You will save processing time if you only rotate a few objects.

16. Do not try to **edit** drawings with **perspective** mode **ON**. Editing and drawing are **not** allowed when viewing a model in perspective.

17. To make **edits** to **perspective views, save the perspective view** first with the **VIEW** command. Then return to the PLAN view or any other viewpoint and make all the desired changes. Then **restore** the **saved view** with the **VIEW** command and the changes made will be reflected in the restored perspective view.

18. Do not use the **DVIEW** option **Distance** in place of the ZOOM command. The **DVIEW Distance** option is used to view a model by setting the CAMERA and TARGET distances so you can view it in perspective. Use the AutoCAD ZOOM command or the ZOOM option within the DVIEW command to magnify your view.

19. Never try to **draw** or **edit** when you see a "broken pencil" icon in the lower left corner of the screen or viewport. The "broken pencil" icon indicates that the viewpoint you are looking at has the drawing situated in such a way that it does not accurately display the current UCS; therefore when drawing or editing, you can get very peculiar results. When you see the "broken pencil" icon, say "What you see is not necessarily what you get".

20. When **dimensioning** in 3D, make sure you are aware of what UCS is current and **place dimensions** aligned to one of the drawings **entities or UCSs.** Use the **UCS Entity** or **UCS 3Point** option to place dimensions. Also make sure to use the AutoCAD **OSNAPS** for placing all dimensions.

21. Make sure to **set** the **UCS** back to **WORLD** before using the **DVIEW** command. The DVIEW CAMERA and TARGET angles will not be accurate if the UCS is not set back to the WCS. The AutoCAD **system variable** called **WORLDVIEW** is set to **1** and automatically brings you back to the **WCS** as you **enter** the **DVIEW** command. As you **exit** the **DVIEW** command, you are automatically set to **UCS Previous**. If you are having problems orientating your view with the DVIEW command, you should check the WORLDVIEW system variable and make sure it is set at 1.

22. Make sure to **set** the **UCS** back to **WORLD** before **plotting**. You can have unusual problems while trying to plot from a user-defined coordinate system.

23. The **BLOCK** and **WBLOCK** commands can be used to place **multiple views** of an object on the same drawing or different drawings if required. Any view of any object on any drawing can be saved as a BLOCK or WBLOCK and then placed on any drawing. To do so, first **create** the desired **view** with the **DVIEW or VPOINT** command and then change the **UCS** to **View**. Next **create** the **BLOCK or WBLOCK** with an appropriate name. Then you can insert each of the blocks on any other UCS or plane. You must, however, **set** the **UCS** to **View** before creating the BLOCK; otherwise the BLOCK will be inserted parallel to the current UCS, which may not give the desired result.

☞ **NOTE:** When a 3D drawing is **WBLOCKed**, the current UCS becomes the WCS and all UCSs, named views, and saved viewport configurations are deleted from the WBLOCK file.

SUMMARY

The completed 3D model can be enhanced by adding colors and shadows on the surfaces with AutoDESK's shading program AutoSHADE.

Chapter 7 will explain how to create a shaded model by placing a CAMERA and LIGHTS using all of the AutoSHADE commands. Script files to put the shaded images in motion on the screen will also be discussed.

AUTOSHADE

INTRODUCTION TO AUTOSHADE

AutoSHADE is a separate software package which supplements AutoCAD. It can be used to render AutoCAD three-dimensional drawings into shaded surface models to provide the user with a better representation of the completed model. Rendering a 3D model means to apply such properties as color, shadowing detail, or texture.

AutoSHADE is used after the 3D drawing is completed within AutoCAD. Any drawing done with AutoCAD Version 2.6 or higher can be shaded with AutoSHADE. You must exit the AutoCAD drawing editor after completing the 3D wireframe model and placing the CAMERA and LIGHTS; then enter into the AutoSHADE program.

You probably have noticed that the wireframe models designed inside AutoCAD can become somewhat confusing to visualize as the drawing gets complex. The HIDE command provides a solution to the problem by removing the lines hidden behind certain surfaces. AutoSHADE goes one step further and creates a shaded image from the wireframe model which is much more realistic.

The images created with AutoSHADE provide the designer with the ability to view a three-dimensional model as a true surface model without having to build expensive prototypes. Shaded images are much more clearly defined than wireframe images.

AUTOSHADE CONFIGURATION

Before you actually configure AutoSHADE, be sure that you make backup copies of your original AutoSHADE disks, then copy all the files from your AutoSHADE disks to the hard drive of your computer. You can make a separate directory for AutoSHADE, but it is recommended that you place all of the AutoSHADE files directly into the ACAD directory. This will make the installation and operation much simpler.

If you are not sure how to install the AutoSHADE software or need to create a SHADE subdirectory, refer to the AutoSHADE users' guide from AutoDESK for the procedure.

Once the software is loaded onto the hard drive of your computer, AutoSHADE will need to be configured for the type of hardware you have.

If you are using any AutoDESK Device Interface (ADI) drivers with AutoSHADE, you should install them before configuring AutoSHADE. You must also physically install the hardware to be used such as a mouse or printer before configuration. You will have problems if you try to load the drivers before actually installing the hardware on to your machine. To fully utilize the graphics board and monitor with AutoSHADE make sure to look at the AutoSHADE users' guide and the reference manual for the particular graphics board in your machine.

Make sure to check the AutoSHADE users' guide for the complete procedure for installing and configuring the AutoSHADE program.

If you are familiar with computers and loading software, the simple procedure below can be used for installing AutoSHADE.

1. Make backup copies of all the AutoSHADE program disks.

2. From the DOS prompt type **CD\ACAD** to change to the ACAD (AutoCAD) directory.

3. Copy all the AutoSHADE program files to the **ACAD** directory on the computer's hard drive.

4. Configure AutoSHADE. From the DOS prompt line type **SHADE**.

5. Follow the prompts that appear on the screen and answer all the questions. The first prompt will ask for you to select a **pointing device**. Select the appropriate pointing device. The next prompt will ask you to select a **display device**. Select the correct display device. Then you will be asked to select a **rendering display device** (check the AutoSHADE users guide to determine what rendering device to use). Select the same rendering device as the display device.

6. You will then be asked if you have a single screen or a dual screen. Make sure you answer this question correctly. Type Y for a single screen.

7. Finally, you will be asked to choose a **hard copy device**. Select the rendering hard copy device to be used (printer or plotter). For example select **2:Postscript device.**

8. When you have completed the AutoSHADE configuration, the AutoSHADE interactive screen and menu bar will appear.

9. Move the mouse or pointing device around on the screen. If it does not move, you will have to reconfigure AutoSHADE again. To do so, first delete the **SHADE.CFG** file from the **C:\ACAD** directory and then start at step 4.

   If you don't have a mouse configured, you will have to use the arrow keys on the keyboard. Press the **[UP]** arrow key and move the arrow over to the word **File**, then press the **[INSERT]** key to select the item, not the **[ENTER]** key.

10. To **exit** AutoSHADE, bring the arrow to the word **File at the top of the screen and "pick"** (or use the **[INSERT]** key). Scroll down the pull-down window and highlight **Quit,** then **"pick"** with the pointing device.

HARDWARE AND SOFTWARE REQUIREMENTS

The AutoSHADE program requirements are:

- IBM PC or PS/2 family computer or compatible
- 640K RAM
- Math coprocessor (8087, 80287, 80387)
- Hard drive
- Supported video display and adapter (CGA, VGA, EGA)
- Supported pointing device (mouse, etc.)
- AutoSHADE program files
- Supported operating system (DOS)
- AutoCAD program files
- Hard copy rendering device (optional)

☞   NOTE: Make sure you have the proper settings for the **ACADFREERAM, LISPHEAP,** and **LISPSTACK** variables to be placed in the **Autoexec.bat** file.

The following lines can be placed in the Autoexec.bat file:

SET ACADFREERAM=24000
SET LISPHEAP=39000
SET LISPSTACK=6000

The LISPHEAP and LISPSTACK combined total should not exceed 45000.

AUTOSHADE COMMANDS

There are two sets of AutoSHADE commands. First, there are the AutoSHADE commands which actually control the rendering of the drawing inside the AutoSHADE program. These are the commands used to actually shade a model. These AutoShade program commands can be accessed only from the pull-down window selections at the top of the screen inside the AutoSHADE program. This is called the **AutoSHADE interactive display,** illustrated in Fig. 7-1. This is the screen which will be displayed once you are inside the AutoSHADE program.

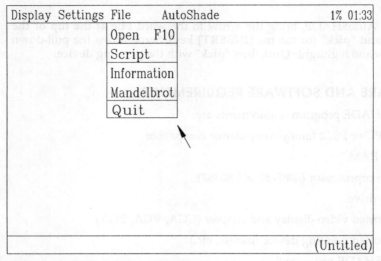

Figure 7-1 AutoSHADE interactive display.

The very top line in the **AutoSHADE interactive display** is called the menu bar and it contains the pull-down windows available for you to access the AutoSHADE commands. You cannot type commands in at the keyboard while using AutoSHADE.

These AutoSHADE program commands will be discussed in detail after we create a drawing inside AutoCAD and then import it into AutoSHADE.

Secondly, there are the AutoSHADE commands inside the AutoCAD program which allow you to set up the shading environment of the drawing created in AutoCAD before it is imported into AutoSHADE.

These commands can be found in the AutoCAD drawing editor by selecting **Options,** then **Ashade** from the pull-down windows. These commands will allow you to place a **CAMERA** and **LIGHT sources** around the drawing to set up the shading environment.

USING AUTOSHADE

The following pages will describe how to create a three-dimensional model with AutoCAD and then use the AutoSHADE commands to place a **CAMERA** and **LIGHTS,** set up a **scene** and create a **FILMROLL** file which can then be imported into AutoSHADE for rendering.

AutoSHADE is a very complex program with many commands which will require you to think in 3D. The exercise that follows will take you step by step through the whole process of creating the drawing in AutoCAD and then bringing it into AutoSHADE so you can see it shaded. You will be able to create tremendous visual effects with AutoSHADE from any 3D model designed inside AutoCAD and will find it a valuable tool for displaying your 3D models.

GETTING STARTED

Try creating a simple 3D wireframe model within AutoCAD and then shade it with AutoSHADE. Start AutoCAD. From the AutoCAD main menu select **1** **"Begin a NEW drawing"**. Name the drawing "SHADE1".

Use the procedure shown below to set up the following drawing parameters:

UNITS	Decimal
2 Decimal Places
Decimal Degrees
2 Fractional Places For Displaying Angles
East = 3 O'clock
Angles Measured Counter Clockwise

LIMITS	Lower Left = 0,0
Upper Right = 36,24

☞   NOTE: The [ENTER] key can be used to select the AutoCAD default values.

From the command prompt line enter the **UNITS** command.

❖ **Command:**UNITS

The following is displayed:

System of units	Examples
1. Scientific	1.55E+01
2. Decimal	15.50
3. Engineering	1'-3.50"
4. Architectural	1'-3 1/2"
5. Fractional	15 1/2

Enter choice, 1 to 5 <2>:
type **2 [ENTER]**
Number of digits to right of
decimal point (0 to 8) <4>:
type **2 [ENTER]**

The UNITS command proceeds to angles and displays the following menu:

Systems of angle measure:	(Examples)
1. Decimal degrees	45.0000
2. Degrees/minutes/seconds	45d0'0"
3. Grads	50.0000g

4. Radians   0.7854r

5. Surveyor's units   N45d0'0" E

Enter choice, 1 to 5 <1>:
type **1 [ENTER]**
Number of fractional places for display of angles <0 to 8>:
type **2 [ENTER]**

After selecting the angle format, the following prompt will appear:

Direction for angle 0:

East	3 o'clock	= 0.00
North	12 o'clock	= 90.00
West	9 o'clock	= 180.00
South	6 o'clock	= 270.00

Enter direction for angle <0.00 >:
press **[ENTER]**

After selecting the angle 0 direction, you'll receive the prompt:

Do you want angles measured clockwise<N>:

press **[ENTER]**

Next you should set the **limits**. Type the LIMITS command.

❖ **Command:**LIMITS
ON/OFF/<Lower left corner> <0.00 ,0.00>:
press **[ENTER]** for lower left corner
Upper right corner<12.00,9.00>:
type **36,24 [ENTER])**

Flip back to the drawing screen. Press the **[F1]** key.

Enter the ZOOM command. Type **ZOOM.**

❖ **Command:**ZOOM
All/Center/Dynamic/Extents/
Left/Prev/Window/<Scale(X)>:
type **A [ENTER]**

This allows you to view the entire limits of the drawing.

Set the **GRID** size to 1 using the GRID command. Type GRID **and press
[ENTER]**.

❖ **Command:**GRID
Grid spacing(X) or ON/OFF/Snap/Aspect<0.00>:
type **1 [ENTER]**

Set the **SNAP** to 1 using the SNAP command. Type SNAP and press **[ENTER]**.

❖ **Command:**SNAP
Snap spacing or ON/OFF/Aspect/Rotate/Style <1.00>:
type **1 [ENTER]**

DRAWING THE MODEL

Let's draw a basic 3D model. Draw the shapes shown here (Fig. 7-2). Use the LINE command with SNAP ON to draw the two rectangles somewhere near the center of the screen in the World Coordinate System. Make sure that all the corners are closed. The sizes of the rectangles are not that important but should be proportional the ones shown here.

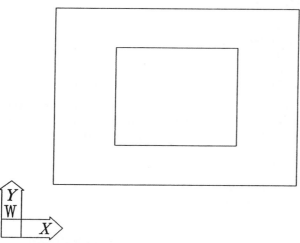

Figure 7-2 Drawing the model.

Cancel out of the LINE command and use the CHANGE command to change the **elevation** and **thickness** of the rectangles. Type CHANGE.

❖ **Command:**CHANGE
Select objects:
pick the larger rectangle only **[ENTER]**
Properties/<Change point>:
type **P [ENTER]**
Change what Property (Color/Elev
/LAyer/LType/Thickness)?:
type **TH** for thickness **[ENTER]**
New Thickness<0.00>:
type **1 [ENTER]**
press **[ENTER]** again to exit the CHANGE command.

Reenter the **CHANGE** command (press the space bar or the **[ENTER]** key) and change the smaller rectangle to a **thickness** of 1.5 and an **elevation** of 1. You can use the **[ENTER]** key or use the **[SPACE BAR]** to repeat the CHANGE command.

> ❖ **Command:**CHANGE
> *Select objects:*
> pick the small rectangle **[ENTER]**
> *Properties/<Change point>:*
> type **P [ENTER]**
> *Change what Property(Color/Elev*
> */LAyer/LType/Thickness)?:*
> type **TH** for thickness **[ENTER]**
> *New Thickness<0.00>:*
> type **1.5 [ENTER]**
> *Change what Property(Color/Elev*
> *LAyer/LType/Thickness)?:*
> type **E** for Elevation **[ENTER]**
> *New Elevation<0.00>:*
> type **1 [ENTER]**
> press **[ENTER]** again to exit the CHANGE command.

Select **DISPLAY** from the pull-down windows. Then select **VPOINT 3D...** Now select with the arrow the viewpoint option in the lower right corner of the dialogue box (FRONT/RIGHT). The command prompt line displays:

> ❖ **Command:**VPOINT
> *Rotate/<View point<0.00,0.00,1.00>:R*
> *Enter angle in X-Y plane from X axis <270>:<315*
> *Enter angle from X-Y plane <90.00>:*
> type **30,** then **[ENTER]**

Use the ZOOM command to reduce the size of the display. Type ZOOM.

> ❖ **Command:**ZOOM
> *All/Center/Dynamic/Extents/*
> *Left/Prev/Window/<Scale(X)>:*
> type **.7x [ENTER]**

The display should look something like Fig. 7-3.

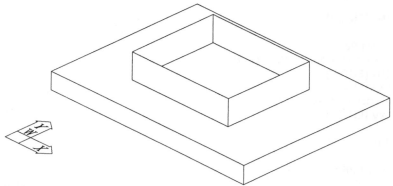

Figure 7-3 3D wireframe rectangles.

The **thickness** option sets the **height** of each of the rectangles. The **elevation** option raises the base point of the smaller rectangle to an elevation of **1**.

Now we are going to draw a pyramid on the top of the small rectangle (Fig. 7-4). Select **DRAW** from the pull-down windows. Next scroll down the window and select **3D Construction....**

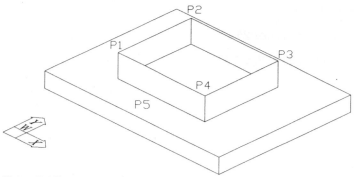

Figure 7-4 Drawing a pyramid on top.

Move the arrow over to the action box to the left of the **pyramid** and "pick". AutoCAD prompts:

Please wait... Loading 3D Objects.
First base point:
type **INT [ENTER]**
of
pick point **P1** (Fig. 7-4)
Second base point:
type **INT [ENTER]**
of
pick point **P2**
Third base point:

type **INT [ENTER]**
of
pick point **P3**
Tetrahedron/<Fourth base point>:
type **INT [ENTER]**
pick point P4
Ridge/Top/ <Apex point>:
type **.xy [ENTER]**
of
type **MID**
of
pick point **P5**
of (need Z):
type **6 [ENTER]**

☞   NOTE: Make sure to use the AutoCAD OSNAPS when picking all
           points.

Use the HIDE command to remove hidden lines. Type **HIDE**.

❖ **Command:**HIDE
    Regenerating drawing.
    Removing hidden lines:25

The drawing should look like Fig. 7-5 .

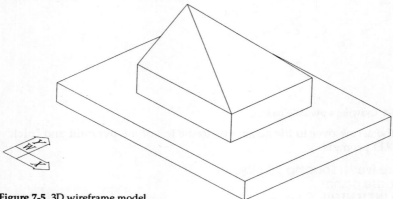

Figure 7-5 3D wireframe model.

Now we will draw a 3DFACE on the top of the large rectangle with the 3DFACE
command (Fig. 7-6).

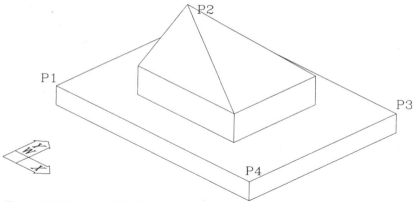

Figure 7-6 Drawing a 3DFACE.

From the AutoCAD root screen menu at the right, select **3D**. Then select **3DFACE**. AutoCAD prompts:

❖ **Command:**3DFACE
   First point:
   type **INT [ENTER]**
   pick point **P1** (Fig. 7-6)
   Second point:
   type **INT [ENTER]**
   pick point **P2**
   Third point:
   type **INT [ENTER]**
   pick point **P3**
   Fourth point:
   type **INT [ENTER]**
   pick point P4
   Third point:

Press **[ENTER]** to exit the 3DFACE command after selecting point P4.

Use the HIDE command again to remove hidden lines. Type HIDE.

❖ **Command:**HIDE
   Regenerating drawing.
   Removing hidden lines:25

Notice the difference in the result of the HIDE command after creating the 3DFACE on the top of the large rectangle (Fig. 7-7).

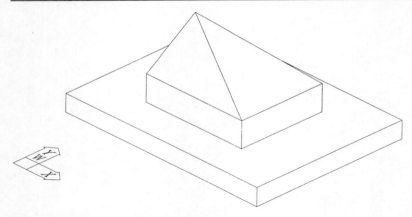

Figure 7-7 Hiding lines to complete the model.

ADDING COLOR

Now use the CHANGE command to change the color of the pyramid on the top to **BLUE**. Type CHANGE.

❖ **Command:**CHANGE
Select objects:
pick the top of the pyramid, then press **[ENTER]**
Properties/<Change point>:
type **P [ENTER]**
Change what Property(Color/Elev
/LAyer/LType/Thickness)?:
type **C** for color **[ENTER]**
New color <BYLAYER>:
type **BLUE [ENTER]**.
press **[ENTER]** again to exit the CHANGE command.

Use the CHANGE command again to change the color of the 3DFACE on the top of the large rectangle to RED. Type CHANGE or press the space bar.

❖ **Command:**CHANGE
Select objects:
pick the **3DFACE** just created on the large rectangle, then
[ENTER]
Properties/<Change point>:
type **P [ENTER]**
Change what Property(Color/Elev
/LAyer/LType/Thickness)?:
type **C** for color **[ENTER]**
New color <BYLAYER>:
type **RED [ENTER]**.
press **[ENTER]** again to exit the CHANGE command.

Save the drawing at this point with the AutoCAD SAVE command. Do not exit the drawing editor. Type **SAVE.**

❖ **Command:**SAVE
 File name <SHADE1>:
 press **[ENTER]** to select the default file name **"SHADE1".**

ADDING LIGHTS

Now try to shade the wireframe model with AutoSHADE. First, you should reduce the size of the display to get the object smaller and in the center of the screen so we can place a **CAMERA** and some **LIGHTS** with the **AutoSHADE** commands. Use the ZOOM command. Type ZOOM.

❖ **Command:**ZOOM
 All/Center/Dynamic/Extents/
 Left/Prev/Window/<Scale(X)>:
 type **.5X [ENTER]**

The drawing may look rather small, but that is OK. Turn the GRIDS ON. Press **[F7]**. The GRID boundaries indicate the overall paper size.

Now we are ready to create the shaded image. From the pull-down windows select **Options.** Then select **Ashade....**

AutoCAD prompts:

 Please wait... Loading ashade.

You will now see the ASHADE dialogue box (Fig. 7-8). This is the first set of AutoSHADE commands which allow us to set up the shading environment.

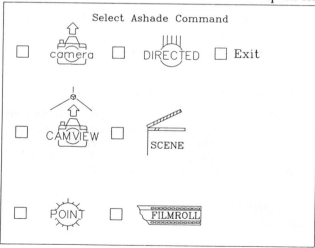

Figure 7-8 ASHADE dialogue box.

Move the arrow around in the dialogue box and select the icon **DIRECTED**. This is a LIGHT source that can be directed at the object to produce shadows. AutoCAD now prompts:

Enter a light name:
Enter a name.
Type **L1** for LIGHT 1, then **[ENTER]**.
Point source or Directed <P>:
Enter light aim point:
Pick a point at about point **P1** with the pointing device (Fig. 7-9).

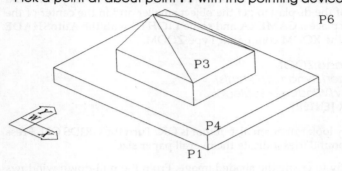

Figure 7-9 Adding the CAMERA and lights.

AutoCAD now prompts:

Enter light location:

Pick a point way outside the paper at about point **P2** (Fig. 7-9).

After you have picked a location for the first LIGHT, AutoCAD will place an icon (on the X-Y plane) of a small directed LIGHT source pointing at the aim point picked and then take you back to the ASHADE command dialogue box where you can select another option. Let's place another LIGHT on the object. Move the arrow to select the icon **POINT** and "pick". AutoCAD prompts:

Enter a light name:
type **L2** for LIGHT 2, then **[ENTER]**.
Point source or Directed <P>:
Enter light location:
type **.xy [ENTER]**
of

Pick near the center point of the bottom rectangle **P3** (Fig. 7-9).
of (need Z):
type **8 [ENTER]**

This will place a point LIGHT source **eight** units above the center of the object. You will notice that small **Light** icons appear on the drawing to indicate approximately where the LIGHTS have been placed.

After you place the LIGHTS, AutoCAD will take you back to the ASHADE command dialogue box. You can place as many LIGHTS as you like in the same manner. For this example we will only use two, **L1** and **L2**.

PLACING A CAMERA

You can place a **CAMERA** somewhere on the drawing as if you were to take a snapshot of the object at the angle it is rotated on the screen with the LIGHTS placed as shown (Fig. 7-9). Move the arrow in the dialogue box to select the icon **CAMERA** and "pick". AutoCAD prompts:

Enter camera name:
type **CAM1 [ENTER]**
Enter target point:
type **INT [ENTER]**
of

Pick the point **(P4)** of intersection at the top front corner of the large rectangle (Fig. 7-9).
Enter camera location:
type **.xy [ENTER]**
of

Pick a point at about point **P5** (Fig. 7-9) outside the drawing limits.
of (need Z):
type **2 [ENTER]**

This places the CAMERA two units above the X-Y plane outside the drawing LIMITS at the point picked. A small icon of a camera is displayed at the selected location. The CAMERA should be placed away from the object so you will be able to view the entire object.

After you place the **CAMERA**, AutoCAD will take you back to the ASHADE command dialogue box again. You can place several CAMERAS if you like. For this example we will only use the one CAMERA.

CREATING A SCENE

Now you need to create what is called a **scene**. The scene will contain the information and locations for the CAMERA and LIGHT sources. From the ASHADE dialogue box select the **scene** icon. AutoCAD prompts:

Enter scene name:
Type a name for the scene. Type **SC1** for scene 1, then **[ENTER]**.
AutoCAD now prompts:

Select the camera:
Pick the **CAMERA** icon on the drawing with the pointing device.
Next AutoCAD prompts:

Select a light:
Pick the first LIGHT you placed **(L1)** with the pointing device
(DIRECTED LIGHT).

Select a light:
Pick the second LIGHT you placed **(L2)** with the pointing device
(POINT LIGHT).

You can keep on picking LIGHTS if you have more located on the drawing or
you can simply press **[ENTER]** to exit to the next prompt.

Select a light:
Press **[ENTER]** to continue when finished selecting all LIGHTS.
AutoCAD now prompts:
Enter scene location:
Pick at about point **P6** (Fig. 7-9).

A small clipboard displaying the scene name, CAMERA name and LIGHT
names is placed at the point you picked. You can place the scene clipboard
anywhere on the drawing away from the object.

The drawing should now look like Fig. 7-10:

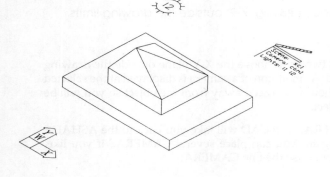

Figure 7-10 Shading environment.

PRODUCING THE FILMROLL

Now you have placed the **CAMERA** and **LIGHTS** and are ready to create the shaded image. First, you must create a file from the drawing that you have on the screen in order to import it into AutoSHADE.

From the pull-down windows select **Options**. Then select **Ashade...** again. When the ASHADE dialogue box appears, "pick" the icon **FILMROLL** at the bottom of the dialogue box. AutoCAD prompts:

Enter Filmroll file name <SHADE1>:

Type in a filename to be used to import into AutoSHADE. You can accept the default drawing name shown in the brackets by pressing the [ENTER] key.

AutoCAD now creates a **FILMROLL file** which can be imported into AutoSHADE. The file will have the name that you gave with an extension of .FLM. For this example, the name would be **SHADE1.FLM**.

The AutoCAD prompt line will echo the message:

"Creating Filmroll file"
Processing face:17
Filmroll created

The file will be located in the ACAD directory and it has all the properties as the drawing does including the features needed for shading such as the **LIGHTS, CAMERA,** and **SCENE**.

The drawing cannot actually be shaded from inside the AutoCAD drawing editor. You must exit AutoCAD and enter the AutoSHADE program. But, first you should save the drawing inside AutoCAD.

Use the **SAVE** command again to save the drawing with the default file name. Type **SAVE**, then [ENTER].

❖ **Command:**SAVE
 File name <SHADE1>:
 press **[ENTER]**

Exit the AutoCAD drawing editor. Use the **QUIT** command. Type **QUIT**.

❖ **Command:**QUIT
 Really want to discard all changes to drawing?
 type **YES [ENTER]**

When you see the AutoCAD main menu on the screen, select item **0 Exit AutoCAD**. This will exit you to the DOS prompt.

THE AUTOSHADE INTERACTIVE SCREEN

At this point you should be at the DOS prompt and inside the ACAD directory of your computer's C: drive. If you followed the instructions for loading the

AutoSHADE program from the beginning of this chapter, all of the program files needed to run **AutoSHADE** are located inside the ACAD directory. If you created a separate directory for AutoSHADE, then you will need to change to that directory in order to run AutoSHADE.

To load and run AutoSHADE, type **SHADE** at the DOS prompt, then press **[ENTER]**. If the program is properly configured for your computer, you will see the following screen (Fig. 7-11):

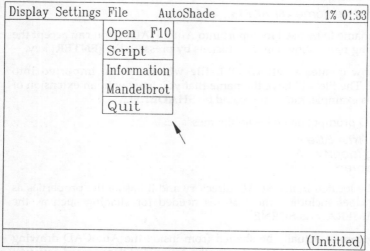

```
Display Settings File        AutoShade                    1% 01:33
                  ┌──────────────┐
                  │ Open    F10  │
                  │ Script       │
                  │ Information  │
                  │ Mandelbrot   │
                  │ Quit         │
                  └──────────────┘
                          ↖




 ─────────────────────────────────────────────────────
                                              (Untitled)
```

Figure 7-11 AutoSHADE interactive display.

☞ **NOTE:** If AutoSHADE does not seem to load properly, check the AutoSHADE users' guide for proper installation and setup.

This screen is called the **AutoSHADE interactive screen.** It works the same way as the pull-down windows inside the AutoCAD drawing editor.

If you do not have a **mouse** connected to your computer, you will need to use the **arrow keys** at the keyboard to move the **arrow pointer** on the screen to select a command. The AutoSHADE commands cannot be typed in at the keyboard as they can be typed inside the AutoCAD drawing editor. For example, move the **arrow pointer** on the screen up to the top line of the screen with the mouse or keyboard **[UP]** arrow key. Highlight the word **File** and pick with the left button on the pointing device. If you are using the keyboard, press the **[INSERT]** key when the arrow on the screen is over the word **File**. A pull-down window (Fig. 7-11) is displayed with some of the AutoSHADE commands. Now move the **arrow pointer** on the screen to the word **Settings** and select it. You will see some more AutoSHADE commands. Now move the **arrow pointer** over to the word **Display** and select it. These are the three pull-down windows for inputting all of the AutoSHADE commands.

☞   NOTE: If you are not using a mouse, use the [INSERT] key to select.
Notice also that some of the commands can be activated
with the **function** keys [F1] through [F10]. Also some of the
commands can be activated by using the [ALT] key in conjunction with a **function** key. The function and [ALT] keys are
listed next to the commands in the pull-down windows.

When the arrow points to a item on the top line or menu bar the item is
highlighted. When you pick the highlighted item a window with the
AutoSHADE commands appear. You can scroll down in the windows or use
the **function** or [ALT] and **function** keys to activate the desired command.

If a selection is **grayed out,** it means that the command is not available for you
to use at the present time. If you do not want to make any selection and would
like to clear the screen of the pull-down windows, just place the arrow pointer
in a blank area of the screen and **pick** or just press the [ESC] key.

Occasionally you will see dialogue boxes appear on the screen as they do inside
the AutoCAD drawing editor. You can make selections inside the dialogue
boxes with the arrow pointer as you do with AutoCAD. If you are using the
keyboard as your only input device, place the arrow pointer over the item
desired with the arrow keys and select it by pressing the [INSERT] key, not the
[ENTER] key.

☞   NOTE: If you are working with the keyboard the [PAGE UP] and
[PAGE DOWN] keys on the keyboard will change the incre-
mental distance the pointer will move on the screen. The
[PAGE UP] key increases the distance and speed. The
[PAGE DOWN] key reduces the distance and speed. The
[HOME] key moves the arrow to the upper left of the screen.

If you are using a mouse, place the arrow pointer in the desired item and **pick.**
To exit a dialogue box select **OK** or **CANCEL** from the bottom of the dialogue
box. You will see a dialogue box in the next section.

LOADING THE FILMROLL

To begin the shading process with AutoSHADE, we need first to load a file to
shade. The types of files that can be loaded are created in the AutoCAD drawing
editor after positioning the **CAMERA** and **LIGHTS**.

The very last thing we did in AutoCAD was to create a **FILMROLL** file from
the drawing with the **CAMERA** and **LIGHTS** placed in position. Once inside
the AutoSHADE interactive screen, we can load the file we created.

Move the arrow pointer to the top line on the screen and select **File.** Remember
to use the [INSERT] key for selecting items when using the keyboard as your
only input device. Now scroll down the window and select **Open** or press the

[F10] function key to open a **FILMROLL** file. The following **Select filmroll file** dialogue box appears (Fig. 7-12):

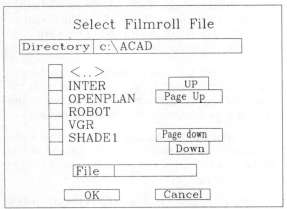

Figure 7-12 Select filmroll dialogue box.

Notice the directory name listed at the top of the dialogue box.

There should be a listing of FILMROLL files on the left side of the dialogue box. All of the files may not be shown. Place the arrow pointer on the option **DOWN** and **pick** to scroll down the file listing. The **UP** option will scroll back up the file listing one line at a time. The **PAGE UP** or **PAGE DOWN** screen options will scroll up or down a whole screen one page at a time.

Scroll down the FILMROLL file listing by placing the arrow pointer on the **DOWN** option and pick continuously until you see the FILMROLL file called **SHADE1**. This is the FILMROLL file which you created from within AutoCAD.

Now move the arrow pointer over to the box just to the left of the file **SHADE1** and **pick**. The filename should now appear in the **File** box. Now move the arrow pointer to select **OK** at the bottom of the dialogue box and **pick**. At the bottom of the screen is the AutoSHADE status line. It should read:

Reading Filmroll file.

The name of the FILMROLL file also appears on the bottom right corner of the screen. Another dialogue box will appear. This is the **Select Scene** dialogue box (Fig. 7-13). The Select Scene dialogue box works the same way as the **Select Filmroll** dialogue box.

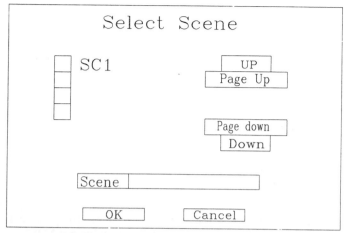

Figure 7-13 Select scene dialogue box.

SELECTING THE SCENE

You will now need to select a **scene**. The scene determines the locations and angles of the LIGHTS and CAMERA. There can be several scenes listed for each FILMROLL file. The scenes are created in the AutoCAD drawing editor by placing CAMERAS and LIGHTS on the drawing and then picking them and assigning a **scene** name as you did earlier.

Move the arrow pointer to the left of the box that has the scene name **SC1** and **pick**. The scene name now appears in the scene box at the bottom of the dialogue box. Remember this is the scene name we used inside the drawing called **SHADE1** which included the CAMERA called **CAM1** and the LIGHTS called **L1** and **L2**.

Now move the arrow pointer to the **OK** box and **pick**. The screen is cleared.

LOOKING AT PLAN VIEW

Now that you have loaded the **FILMROLL** file and selected the **scene** to use, we can look at the drawing and its shading environment. The shading environment will show the CAMERA and LIGHTS and their positioning.

Let's take a look. Move the arrow pointer in AutoSHADE to the top of the screen and over to the option **Display** and **pick**. Scroll down the window to the first command called **PLAN View** and **pick** or press the **[F5]** function key. The drawing should look similar to Fig. 7-14.

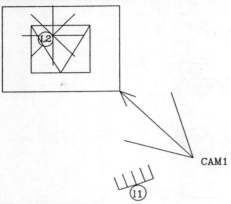

Figure 7-14 PLAN view.

Notice the positioning of the CAMERA and LIGHTS. These are the positions that were chosen in the AutoCAD drawing editor in the drawing **SHADE1**.

LOOKING AT THE WIREFRAME MODEL

Now let's take a look at a 3D wireframe representation of the model with no shading.

Move the arrow pointer to the menu bar at the top of the screen and select **Display** again. Scroll down the window to the command **Wire Frame** and **pick** or press the **[F2]** function key. As the file is being processed, you can see the amount of memory being used at the top right of the screen will increase. The wireframe representation of the model is shown here (Fig. 7-15):

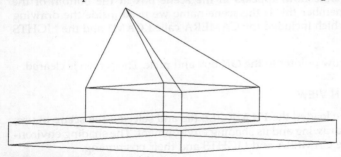

Figure 7-15 Wireframe model.

The drawing is orientated on the display according to the placement and direction of the CAMERA. The CAMERA was placed exactly two units above the front corner of the model. The model is displayed on the screen to the drawing extents.

The wireframe is used to determine if the CAMERA angle is appropriate to achieve the desired result. If the CAMERA angle looks OK, we can make a **FAST SHADE** of the drawing to verify that the lighting is correct.

Now we can shade in the models surfaces or sides.

☞ NOTE: Several messages will appear at the bottom of the screen to let
you know what is happening with the drawing when executing
a **FAST SHADE** or a **FULL SHADE.**

FAST SHADE

The **FAST SHADE** is a quick rendition of what the completed model will look
like, but it may have some flaws. When you execute a **FAST SHADE**, all of the
calculations are not done so you will not get a perfectly shaded image.

To actually render the image with the **FAST SHADE** command move the arrow
pointer to the top of the screen and select **Display** again. Now scroll down the
window and highlight the **Fast Shade** command and **pick** or press the **[F3]**
function key. The object will be shaded according to the locations and directions
of the LIGHT sources and CAMERA (Fig. 7-16).

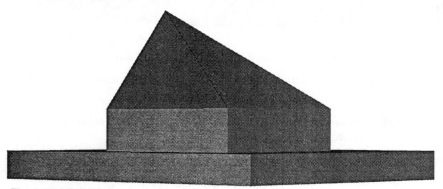

Figure 7-16 FAST SHADE.

Screen monitors are limited to the number of colors that are supported by your
graphics card. The shaded colors shown on the screen may not be exactly the
same as the colors chosen within AutoCAD but should closely resemble the
true color.

A **FAST SHADE** can be done to check the positioning of the LIGHTS and
CAMERA. A **FAST SHADE** is processed much faster then a **FULL SHADE.**

☞ NOTE: The shaded images are dependent also on the hardware
(monitor and video adapter) configuration in your computer.

FULL SHADE

To achieve better results we can execute a **FULL SHADE** on the drawing. This
command will take up more processing time depending on the speed of your
computer.

To get a more accurate rendering of the model move the arrow pointer to the top of the screen and select **Display** again. Now scroll down the window and highlight the **FULL SHADE** command and **pick** or press the **[F4]** function key. The object again will be shaded according to the locations and directions of the LIGHT sources and CAMERA (Fig. 7-17).

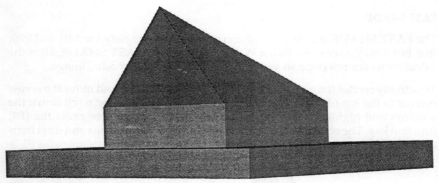

Figure 7-17 FULL SHADE.

Notice the difference in the shaded images of Figs. 7-16 and 7-17.

Notice also the messages that appear at the bottom of the screen in the status line.

☞ NOTE: Be very patient when using the **FULL SHADE** command.
        There is much processing to be done.

This is the AutoCAD shading process with AutoSHADE. You have used some of the **AutoSHADE Display** commands. The next few sections will describe some of the more advanced features of AutoSHADE such as changing the CAMERA angle, ZOOMing in and out, and changing the intensity of the LIGHTS.

REARRANGING THE PICTURE

AutoSHADE has the flexibility of changing the way the shaded image appears on the screen. To change the appearance of the shaded image you can move the CAMERA or the LIGHTS. This can be done two ways, by actually moving the CAMERA and LIGHTS inside the AutoCAD drawing editor with the MOVE command and recreating the FILMROLL file or by using the AutoSHADE commands from within the **AutoSHADE interactive screen**.

The orientation of the image on the screen is determined by the positioning of the LIGHTS and CAMERA from within the AutoCAD drawing editor. You may, however, decide to view the object from another angle, change the position and directions of the LIGHTS or CAMERA, get a closer view, or increase the LIGHT intensities.

ADJUSTING THE CAMERA POSITION

Let's try changing the angle of the CAMERA with the AutoSHADE commands. Move the arrow pointer to the top line of the screen and select **Settings**. Then scroll down the window and select **Camera Position** or press the **[F7]** function key.

The **Camera Specification** dialogue box below appears (Fig. 7-18).

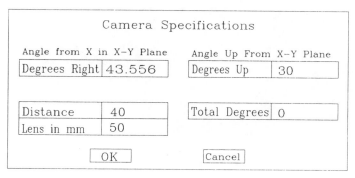

Figure 7-18 Camera specification dialogue box.

Notice the item at the lower left of the dialogue box indicates that the CAMERA has a focal length of 50-mm (millimeters) for the CAMERA's lens. This is what the object would look like if viewed through a CAMERA with a 50-mm lens. The CAMERA angle and distance are also indicated.

Any of these items can be changed by simply placing the arrow pointer in the box with the value to change and typing in a new value. Let's change one of the CAMERA's angles.

Move the arrow pointer to the box with the value that indicates the CAMERA's position in **Degrees up** from the **X-Y plane**. When the box with the existing value is highlighted, type in a new value of **30** and then press **[ENTER]**. Move the arrow pointer over to the box which indicates the CAMERA's **distance** from the object. When the box with the value in it becomes highlighted, type in a new value of **40**, then **[ENTER]**. This moves the CAMERA's position back 40 units and at 30 degrees up from the X-Y plane.

Now move the arrow pointer to the bottom of the dialogue box and select **OK**, then **[ENTER]**.

Now select **Display** from the top of the screen. From the pull-down window scroll down and select **Wire Frame** or press **[F2]**.

Notice that the orientation of the 3D model has changed somewhat.

Move the arrow pointer to the top of the screen again and select **Display**. Now scroll down in the pull-window and select **FULL SHADE** or press the **[F4]** function key.

The object should look like the one below (Fig. 7-19).

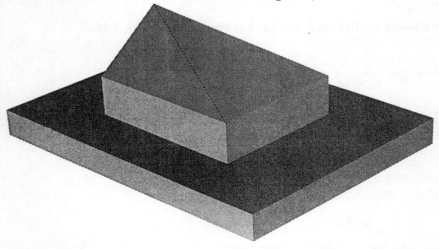

Figure 7-19 FULL SHADE with a new CAMERA position.

☞   **NOTE:** If the shaded image is too high up on the screen, AutoSHADE will clip off the top of the object.

The object can also be rotated in any direction. To rotate the image move the arrow pointer up into the top line of the screen and select **Settings** again. Now scroll down in the pull-down window and select **CAMERA position [F7]** again. In the **CAMERA Specifications** dialogue box (Fig. 7-19) move the arrow pointer to the box which holds the value to indicate the **Degrees right** from **X** in **X-Y plane**. When the box becomes highlighted, type **-80**, then **[ENTER]**.

Now move the arrow pointer to the bottom of the dialogue box and select **OK**.

Now move the arrow pointer back to the top of the screen in the menu bar and select **Display**. Scroll down and select **FULL SHADE** or press **[F4]**. The drawing has now been rotated to a new position (Fig. 7-20).

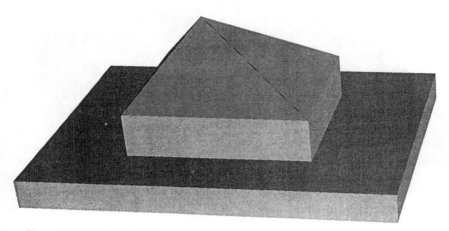

Figure 7-20 FULL SHADE from another angle.

We can also change the **Twist angle** to spin the image around a pivot point on the screen. Move the arrow pointer up into the top line of the screen and select **Settings** again. Now scroll down in the pull-down window and select **CAMERA position** again. In the **Camera Specifications** dialogue box move the arrow pointer to the box which holds the value to indicate the amount of **Twist degrees**. When the box becomes highlighted, type a new value of **15**, then **[ENTER]**.

Move the arrow pointer to the bottom of the dialogue box and select **OK**.

Now move the arrow pointer back to the top of the screen in the menu bar and select **Display**. Scroll down and select **FULL SHADE [F4]**. The drawing has now been rotated again to a new position (Fig. 7-21).

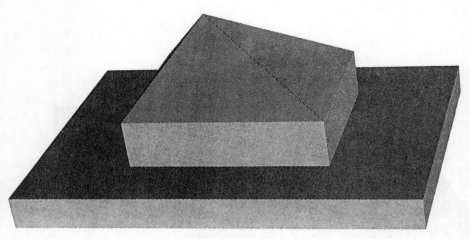

Figure 7-21 FULL SHADE with a new twist angle.

CHANGING THE LENS SIZE

We can also ZOOM in on the image by changing the lens of the CAMERA with the **Lens in mm** option in the **Camera Specification** dialogue box. The larger the focal length of the lens, the closer the object will seem.

Move the arrow pointer up into the top line of the screen and select **Settings** again. Now scroll down in the pull-down window and select **CAMERA position [F7]** again. In the **Camera Specifications** dialogue box move the arrow pointer to the box which holds the value to indicate the size of the lens (Lens in mm). When the box becomes highlighted, type a new value of **75**, then **[ENTER]**.

Move the arrow pointer to the bottom of the dialogue box and select **OK.** Now move the arrow pointer back to the top of the screen in the menu bar and select **Display.** Scroll down and select **FULL SHADE [F4]**. The image becomes enlarged as if viewed from a CAMERA with a 75-mm lens (Fig. 7-22).

Figure 7-22 Changing the CAMERA lens size.

Set the lens length back to **50 mm** with the Camera Specification dialogue box and execute a **FULL SHADE** again by pressing the **[F4]** function key.

Now let's work with the actual shading of the model by adjusting the LIGHTS.

SETTING THE LIGHTS

The brightness of the LIGHTS that we placed on the drawing inside the AutoCAD drawing editor can be adjusted from within the AutoSHADE program.

Move the arrow pointer up into the top line of the screen and select **Settings** again. Now scroll down in the pull-down window and select the **LIGHTS** item. The **Set Light intensities** dialogue box appears (Fig. 7-23).

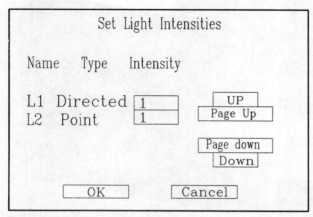

Figure 7-23 Set light intensities dialogue box.

Notice that the two LIGHTS which we defined (L1 and L2) are listed. The LIGHT intensities are set to 1. This is the AutoCAD default. To change the LIGHT intensity just enter a new value for the LIGHT intensity. The larger the value, the brighter the LIGHT. To turn a LIGHT OFF use a value of 0.

Let's make L1, the flood LIGHT, brighter. Move the arrow pointer over the box which contains the value for the LIGHT intensity for L1 (Directed). When the box becomes highlighted, type a new value. Enter a value of 15, press [ENTER], and then select OK at the bottom of the dialogue box.

Produce the shaded image with the new LIGHT intensity set by selecting DISPLAY at the top of the screen and then FULL SHADE or just press the [F4] function key.

Notice the difference between the object now and the object before you changed the LIGHT intensity. The front of the object should be brighter and the side should be darker.

Now change the LIGHT intensity of LIGHT L2 and create the shaded image again with the FULL SHADE command.

There are some other factors which can be changed in the shading environment from within the AutoSHADE interactive display. The CAMERA's location and TARGET points can be changed to produce different views. Perspective mode can be turned ON. A shiny surface model can be created and colors can be changed.

These require more advanced skills and practice with LIGHT and shading but will be discussed here briefly.

ADVANCED SHADING

To experiment with some of the more advanced shading techniques within AutoSHADE, move the arrow pointer to the top of the screen and select **Settings.** Scroll down in the Settings pull-down window and select **Shading Model.** The **Shading Model** dialogue box appears (Fig. 7-24).

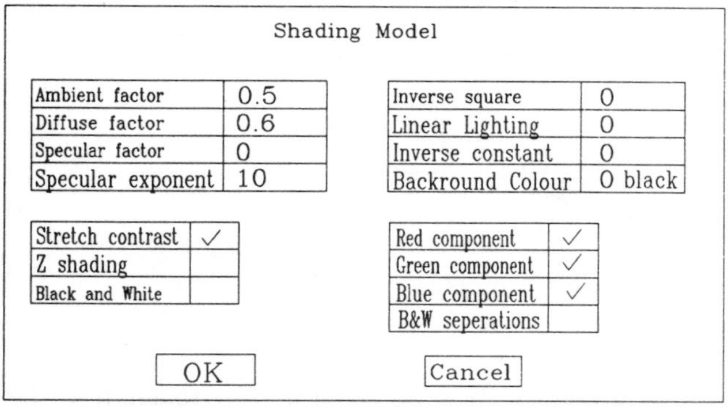

Shading Model			
Ambient factor	0.5	Inverse square	0
Diffuse factor	0.6	Linear Lighting	0
Specular factor	0	Inverse constant	0
Specular exponent	10	Backround Colour	0 black
Stretch contrast	✓	Red component	✓
Z shading		Green component	✓
Black and White		Blue component	✓
		B&W seperations	
OK		Cancel	

Figure 7-24 Shading model dialogue box.

To change the background color of the screen you can move the arrow pointer over to the box which indicates the **Background Color** (Black) and pick. Select a new color by placing a checkmark in the box to the right of the desired color and selecting **OK** at the bottom. Then select **OK** at the bottom of the first dialogue box. Pres **[F4]** for a **FULL SHADE.**

Do not change any of the other items in the **Shading Model** dialogue box right now.

Now select **Settings** from the top of the screen again. Scroll down the window and select **Expert [F8].** The **Expert Specifications** dialogue box appears (Fig. 7-25).

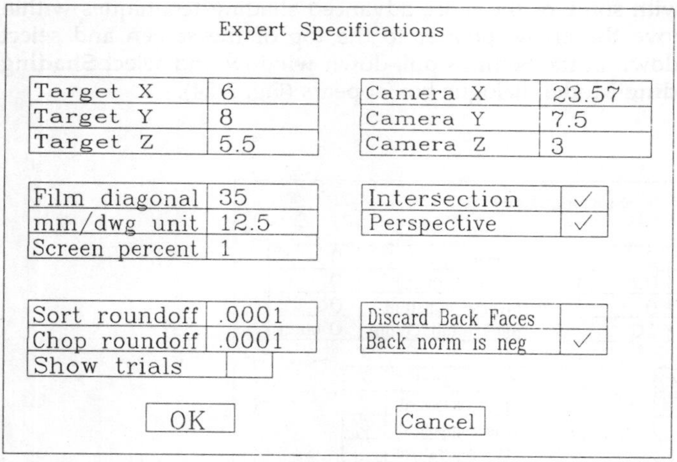

Expert Specifications

Target X	6		Camera X	23.57
Target Y	8		Camera Y	7.5
Target Z	5.5		Camera Z	3

Film diagonal	35		Intersection	✓
mm/dwg unit	12.5		Perspective	✓
Screen percent	1			

Sort roundoff	.0001		Discard Back Faces	
Chop roundoff	.0001		Back norm is neg	✓
Show trials				

OK   Cancel

Figure 7-25 Expert specifications dialogue box.

The **Expert Specifications** dialogue box allows for you to change the CAMERA's position and TARGET point with reference to the World Coordinate System (WCS). You must, however, be aware of the current position of the CAMERA and its angle and be careful when changing these coordinate values. **Perspective** mode can be turned ON and OFF here also. A checkmark in the **Perspective box** indicates that perspective mode is ON. To toggle perspective mode ON and OFF simply place the arrow pointer over the checkmark and pick. You must execute a **FAST** or **FULL SHADE** to see the result after changing to a perspective view.

The **Clipping** command under the **Settings** pull-down window can be used to set clipping points for the display of the rendered image on the screen.

Select **Settings** from the top of the screen. Scroll down the window and select **Statistics**. The **Statistics** command will display a dialogue box with statistics of the rendered image. Select **OK** or press the **[ESC]** key to exit this dialogue box.

To use any of the other items in these dialogue boxes you should fully understand the effects of LIGHT sources on objects, shading, and shadowing. The AutoSHADE users' guide explains these terms in greater detail.

☞ **NOTE:** AutoCAD is not able to produce shadows from the object.

A rendered image from AutoSHADE can be recorded on disk as a separate file of its own and then later displayed on the screen or printer. These files can then be placed together in a script file to create animation or a slide show. Let's create a small slide show of the shaded image being rotated around on the screen.

Before we begin, move the arrow pointer to the top line on the screen and select **File**. Now scroll down the pull-down window and select **Quit**. This will exit you out of AutoSHADE. Now follow the procedure in the next section to create a slide show.

PRODUCING A SHOW

After creating the rendered images as desired within AutoCAD and AutoSHADE, we can redisplay or **Replay** them on the screen individually or one after the other.

Let's start by entering the AutoSHADE program and reloading our FILMROLL file called **SHADE1**.

From the DOS prompt line type **SHADE**.

☞ NOTE: Make sure you are in the AutoCAD directory or in the directory where the AutoSHADE program files are located.

When the **AutoSHADE interactive screen** appears, move the arrow pointer to the top line and select **File**. Scroll down the pull-down window and select **Open** or press **[F10]**. From the **Select filmroll file** dialogue box move the arrow pointer to the **Down** item and pick several times to scroll down in the directory listing until the file called **SHADE1** appears. Select **SHADE1** from the list by moving the arrow pointer to the box to the left of the name and pick. Select **OK** from the bottom of this dialogue box.

Once the FILMROLL file is selected, the **Select scene** dialogue box appears. Select scene **SC1** from the listing of scenes and then select **OK** at the bottom of this dialogue box.

Now move the arrow pointer back to the top of the screen in the menu bar and select **Display**. Scroll down and select **Wire Frame** or press **[F2]**. Select **Display** again from the top of the screen and then scroll down the pull-down window and select **Record** or press the **[ALT]** key in conjunction with the **[F3]** key. This turns **Record** mode **ON**.

As you select **Display** again from the top of the screen, you will notice that there is a checkmark in front of the word **Record**. Now scroll down the window and select **FULL SHADE**. Another dialogue box appears. This is called the **Create rendering replay file** dialogue box (Fig. 7-26). With **Record** mode **ON** you will always get this dialogue box for saving each of the shaded images to disk as a separate file when producing an image.

You need to give a name to the shaded image which will be produced from the model on the screen as it is presently situated and shaded. If you would like to use the default name that appears in the **Filename** box, just pick **OK** at the bottom. This will create a rendering file which will be located on the **C:** drive under the **ACAD** directory. The actual filename would be listed as **SHADE1.RND**.

Create rendering replay file

File name | C:\ACAD\SHADE1

OK   Cancel

Figure 7-26 Create Rendering Replay File Dialogue Box.

Change the name of the rendering file. Move the arrow pointer to the **Filename** item box where the name appears; when the box becomes highlighted, type:

C:\ACAD\SH1

Then press **[ENTER]** or select **OK** from the side of the **Filename** item box. Now select **OK** from the bottom of the dialogue box.

This creates a file in the **C:** drive in the **ACAD** directory with a filename of **SH1.RND**. The actual shaded image will appear on the screen and looks like this (Fig. 7-27):

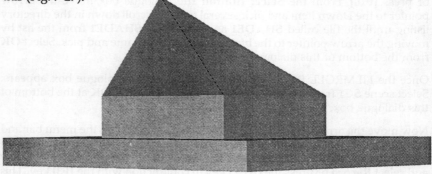

Figure 7-27 Rendered image SH1.RND.

Now create another rendering file with the same drawing rotated slightly on the screen. To do this you will need to change the CAMERA angle.

Move the arrow pointer up to the top of the screen and select **Settings**. Scroll down in the pull-down window and select **CAMERA position**. From the **Camera Specifications** dialogue box move the arrow pointer over the value in the **Distance** item box. When the value for the distance becomes highlighted, type 30, then **[ENTER]**. Then select **OK** from the bottom of this dialogue box.

Select **Display** again and then scroll down to select **FULL SHADE** or press the **[F4]** function key.

In the **Create rendering replay file** dialogue box move the arrow pointer over the **Filename** box and when it becomes highlighted type:

C:\ACAD\SH2 and press [ENTER]

Next select **OK** at the bottom of the dialogue box.

This creates another rendering file which is also located in the **C:** drive in the ACAD directory and has the filename of **SH2.RND**.

The difference between files **SH1.RND** and **SH2.RND** is that the CAMERA is placed further away from the object in the rendering file **SH2.RND**.

Notice the difference in the shaded image (Fig. 7-28):

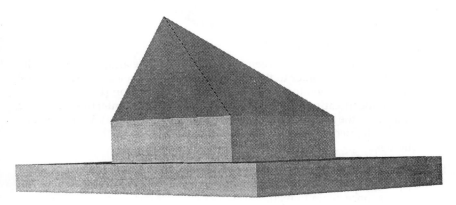

Figure 7-28 Rendered image SH2.RND.

Now rotate the image on the screen and assign another name to this file. Move the arrow pointer to the top of the screen and select **Settings.** Scroll down the pull-down window and select **CAMERA position [F7]** again. From the **Camera Specifications** dialogue box move the arrow pointer over the value which indicates the **Degrees up** (angle up from X-Y plane). When the box becomes highlighted, type **30,** then **[ENTER]**. Select OK from the bottom of the dialogue box.

Select **Display** from the top of the screen again, then scroll down and select **FULL SHADE [F4]**. Change the **filename** in the **Create rendering replay file** dialogue box once again to read:

C:\ACAD\SH3 and press [ENTER]

Select **OK** from the bottom of the dialogue box. The image should now look like Fig. 7-29.

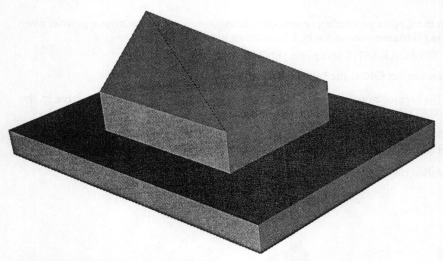

Figure 7-29 Rendered image SH3.RND.

Now rotate the image on the screen to the right and give another name to the file. Move the arrow pointer to the top of the screen and select **Settings**. Scroll down the pull-down window and select **CAMERA position [F7]** again. From the **Camera Specifications** dialogue box move the arrow pointer over the value which indicates the **Degrees right** (angle from X in X-Y plane). When the box becomes highlighted, type **15**, then **[ENTER]**. Select **OK** from the bottom of the dialogue box.

Select **Display** from the top of the screen again, then scroll down and select **FULL SHADE [F4]**. Change the **filename** in the **Create rendering replay file** dialogue box once again to read:

C:\ACAD\SH4 and press **[ENTER]**

Select **OK** from the bottom of the dialogue box.

The image should now look like Fig. 7-30.

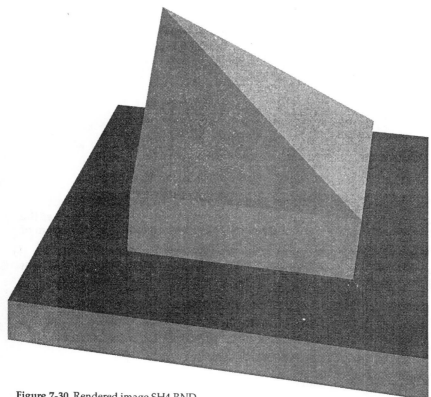

Figure 7-30 Rendered image SH4.RND.

You have now created four separate rendering files within AutoSHADE. Each of them has a distinct **filename** and a file extension of **.RND** in the **C:\ACAD** directory.

We can now look at each one of them separately at any time or we can look at them displayed on the screen one after another as a slide show. Let's try it with the **Replay** command.

Move the arrow pointer to the top of the screen again an select **Display**. Scroll down in the pull-down window and select **Replay** or press the **[ALT]** key in conjunction with the **[F1]** key. Another dialogue box appears (Fig. 7-31).

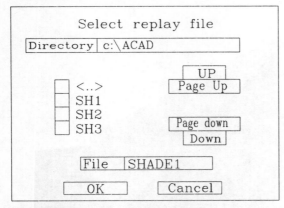

Figure 7-31 Select replay file dialogue box.

This is the **Select Replay file** dialogue box. Move the arrow pointer over the box to the left of the filename **SH1** and pick. Then select **OK** at the bottom of this dialogue box.

The rendering file (SH1.RND) should appear on the screen. Check to see if it looks like Fig. 7-27. You can replay any rendering file you like at any time.

To replay all of the rendering files created at once select **Display** from the top of the screen again, scroll down the pull-down window, and select **Replay All**. Now the **Select Replay Directory** dialogue box appears (Fig. 7-32).

```
┌─────────────────────────────────────────────────┐
│        Select  replay  directory                 │
│ ┌──────────────────────────────────────────────┐ │
│ │Directory│ C:\ACAD                             │ │
│ └──────────────────────────────────────────────┘ │
│   ┌──────────────────────────┬───────────┐       │
│   │Delay  in  Seconds        │     1     │       │
│   └──────────────────────────┴───────────┘       │
│      ┌──────────┐              ┌─────────┐        │
│      │   OK     │              │ Cancel  │        │
│      └──────────┘              └─────────┘        │
└─────────────────────────────────────────────────┘
```

Figure 7-32 Select replay directory dialogue box.

You can change the directory you would like to look through by moving the arrow pointer to the **Directory** item box and typing in the desired directory to search through.

Do not change directories. Search through the directory that already appears in the dialogue box (C:\ACAD).

You can also change the **delay** time between the replaying of the rendering files by changing the value indicated in the **Delay in seconds** item box. Change the value here.

Move the arrow pointer over to highlight the value indicated for **Delay in seconds**. Type in **2**, for 2 seconds, then **[ENTER]**. Now select **OK** from the bottom of the dialogue box.

All of the shaded images which we produced should appear on the screen one at a time with a 2-second delay between each one. Notice that the current rendering filename appears at the lower left corner of the screen in the status line. You will not be able to make another selection with the pointing device until you STOP the replay. To STOP the replay execute a CANCEL by pressing the [CTRL] key in conjunction with the [C] key.

When all the rendering files have been replayed, the last rendered image will be displayed and the arrow pointer will reappear for you to enter another AutoSHADE command.

Now turn **record** mode **off**. Select **Display** from the top of the screen then scroll down and select **Record**. This removes the checkmark from in front of the word **Record** and turns record mode OFF so that no more .RND files are created.

☞ NOTE: Make sure **Record** mode is OFF before trying to produce a hard copy of a shaded image.

Select **File** from the top of the screen in AutoSHADE. Now scroll down and select **Quit** to exit the AutoSHADE program. You should now be at the DOS prompt.

The next section will explain how to use **script** files in AutoSHADE to do the same thing as you did here or to actually execute any of the AutoSHADE commands without even having to enter into the AutoSHADE program commands through the **AutoSHADE interactive screen.**

SCRIPT FILES

Script files can be created to sequentially execute AutoSHADE commands in a batch mode the same way they are used in AutoCAD. A script file is an ASCII text file which can be created with a text editor such as the DOS text editor **EDLIN** or a word processor. AutoSHADE has its own batch files which will make AutoSHADE run automatically.

A script file created with AutoSHADE may be used to produce a series of the same image rotating around the screen to show motion or animation. These script files can be executed from within AutoSHADE by selecting **File** from the top of the screen, then **Script**. Try creating a simple script file to show the object you created rotating on the screen within AutoSHADE.To create the file we will need to use a text editor or word processor. To use the DOS text editor **EDLIN**, at the DOS prompt type:

EDLIN SIMPLE.SCR
New file
*

type **1i [ENTER]**(i to insert line 1)

Type the following lines (do not type the line numbers or the asterisks; EDLIN will cause these to appear). Press [ENTER] after each line.

```
1:*replay sh1
2:*delay 3
3:*replay sh2
4:*delay 3
5:*replay sh3
6:*delay 3
7:*replay sh4
8:*quit
9:*^C                    (press the [CTRL] and [C] keys)
*E                       (type E for END and [ENTER])
```

E will save the script file with the name given above (SIMPLE.SCR).

Now you can execute the script file right from the DOS prompt or you can enter into the AutoSHADE program and execute it.

Try to execute the script file from the DOS prompt first. At the DOS prompt type:

SHADE -SSIMPLE, then press [ENTER]

This will cause the above script file to execute sequentially one command at a time. First AutoSHADE is invoked with the SHADE command at the DOS prompt. The -S tells AutoSHADE to look for a script file and execute it. The name of the script file SIMPLE immediately follows the -S.

The format is:

SHADE -S<script filename>, then [ENTER]

☞ NOTE: There is no space between the -S and the name of the script file. Also, no file extension is needed.

To execute the script file from within AutoSHADE enter the AutoSHADE program by typing in SHADE at the DOS prompt.

Once inside the AutoSHADE interactive screen move the arrow pointer to the top line and select File. Scroll down the pull-down window and select Script. In the Script File dialogue box move the arrow pointer to the blank space for the filename and when it becomes highlighted, type in the path and filename as shown here:

C:\ACAD\SIMPLE

Then press [ENTER]. Select OK from the bottom of the dialogue box. The script file SIMPLE.SCR will be executed as it was before. Notice that no extension is given again for the filename. AutoSHADE automatically knows to look for a script file with the extension of .SCR.

SCRIPT FILE COMMANDS

The following is a list of AutoSHADE file commands that can be used inside script files.

CAMERA <X,Y,Z>	This moves the CAMERA to a new position on the drawing relative to the WCS of the drawing.
DELAY <seconds>	This will cause AutoSHADE to pause for a specified amount of time in seconds.
DISTANCE <dist>	This sets the distance the CAMERA is positioned from the object with reference to its original TARGET point as set within AutoCAD.
DXB <filename>	This creates a DXB file in wireform only.
FASTSHADE <filename>	This performs a FAST SHADE. Make sure to use a filename if record mode or hard copy mode is ON.
FULLSHADE <filename>	This performs a FULL SHADE. The filename is optional unless record or hard copy modes are ON.
HARDCOPY <ON/OFF>	This turns the hardcopy rendering device ON and the display rendering device OFF. The hard copy device must be configured before entering AutoSHADE.
INTERSECTION <ON/OFF>	This toggles intersection checking ON or OFF.
LENS <mm>	This will set the CAMERA lens size to a specified size in millimeters.
OPEN <filmroll>	This will load a new FILMROLL file. No file extension (.FLM) is needed.
PERSPECTIVE <ON/OFF>	This toggles perspective mode ON or OFF.
QUIT	This is used to exit AutoSHADE and to end the script file.
RECORD <ON/OFF>	This is used to turn record mode ON and OFF.
REPLAY <filename>	This will display a recorded rendered file. This is any file with a .RND file extension. The file extension is not needed.
REWIND	This causes AutoSHADE to reexecute the script file from the beginning.
SCENE <name>	This is used to select a scene name.
SLIDE <filename>	This is used create AutoCAD wireframe SLIDE files only.

SPERCENT<number>	This changes the screen percent value.
TARGET <X,Y,Z>	This is used to change the CAMERA target point referenced from the WCS in X, Y, and Z values.
TWIST<angle>	This is used to specify an angle in degrees to change the CAMERA Twist angle.
. comments	The . (period) can be used in the script file to indicate programmer comments.

EXAMPLE SCRIPT FILE

Below is an example script file named **SAMPLE.SCR**. If you are using **EDLIN** to create this file, make sure to use the same conventions as shown in the first example (SIMPLE.SCR).

```
OPEN SHADE1
SCENE SC1
CAMERA 7,5.5,4
RECORD ON
FASTSHADE SH5
FULLSHADE SH6
LENS 75
FULLSHADE SH7
TWIST 15
FULLSHADE SH8
REPLAY SH5
DELAY 2
REPLAY SH6
DELAY 2
REPLAY SH7
DELAY 2
REPLAY SH8
REWIND
```

To execute the script file above from the DOS prompt type:

SHADE -SSAMPLE, then press **[ENTER].**

This script file will OPEN the FILMROLL file called **SHADE1,** select the scene called **SC1,** set the CAMERA point, turn RECORD mode **ON,** execute a **FAST SHADE,** assign the name SH5.RND, then execute a **FULL SHADE,** and assign the name SH6.RND. Next the lens size will change to 75 mm to zoom in on the object, then execute another **FULL SHADE** called SH7.RND. The script file will continue with the TWIST command and actually turn the object on the screen 15 degrees and give it a name of SH8.RND. Finally the script file will REPLAY or redisplay all of the rendering files created from this script file with a DELAY time of 2 seconds between each replay. The REWIND command will reexecute the entire script file from the beginning and cause a continuous loop. To exit the script file you will need to cause a CANCEL (press the [CTRL] and [C] keys).

You can also run AutoSHADE in batch mode from the DOS prompt with a script file. This will eliminate the actual **AutoSHADE interactive screen** and prevent any AutoSHADE messages from appearing on the display. To run the **SIMPLE.SCR** script file we created from the DOS prompt type:

SHADE -B -SSIMPLE, then press **[ENTER]**

Make sure you type in exactly what you see here. The **-b** instructs AutoSHADE to run in batch mode and use a null display driver.

AutoSHADE can be used to produce some very interesting and unique screen images. But it will take time for you to master all of the commands. You must practice working with it.

SUMMARY

You are now able to construct a three-dimensional model within AutoCAD, change your viewpoint and then shade the model's surfaces. The next step after the model is created and shaded is to produce a **Hard Copy** (output) of the drawing.

Chapter 8 will give you some very important tips on how to **plot** a 3D wireframe or surface model. Problems with plotting in 3D are also discussed.

PLOTTING IN 3D

PROBLEMS WITH PLOTTING IN 3D

After you have created your 3D model, you can plot or print it providing you have a supported plotter or printer. Plotting a 3D model may be somewhat confusing and difficult at first. It will take some practice.

If you are using the **DVIEW** or **VPOINT** command and you change your viewpoint of the drawing to a certain angle while in a UCS other than the WCS and then try to plot, you will most likely not get the desired results unless you plot using the **FIT** option from within the PLOT command.

Remember that AutoCAD will change the origin of the plot back to the World Coordinate System (WCS), not the current UCS. This may cause the actual plot origin of the drawing to be wherever it determines the origin to be in the WCS. Therefore the plot origin can be converted to negative values and cause the plot to be way off of the paper.

Do not try to change the plot origin at this point. Before you actually plot you should **always set the UCS back to the WCS, then plot.** The view of the drawing will not change when you are set back to the WCS. Only the UCS icon on the screen will change.

Now when you plot from the WCS, you can determine where the drawing will be positioned on the paper when you execute the first sample plot. You can then make any desired adjustments to the plot origin and rerun the plot to position the drawing at the desired location on the paper. Since the drawing is already using the WCS, no conversion is necessary by AutoCAD.

Remember if you want to HIDE the lines in a wireframe 3D model for the plot, you must answer **YES** to the question:

Remove hidden lines?

in the PLOT command sequence.

Make sure to place **text** and **dimensions** each on separate layers so you can eliminate them from being plotted by either **freezing** or turning them OFF if desired.

PROBLEMS WITH PLOTTING IN 3D

The 3D plotting problems can be very frustrating at first when plotting simple to complex 3D drawings. Some of the problems with plotting 3D objects are listed here. They may be helpful to note before plotting.

1. Lack of control in positioning a 3D drawing on paper.

2. It is very time consuming when plotting 3D models especially when removing hidden lines.

3. 3D views of a plot cannot be rotated 90 degrees clockwise using the option from the plot command. You must rotate your viewpoint of the object with the **VPOINT** or **DVIEW** commands first then execute a plot.

4. You cannot use the HIDE command inside the AutoCAD drawing editor and use the PLOT command to have the hidden lines removed from the plotted output. You must use the **hidden line removal** option from within the PLOT sequence.

5. Hidden line removal will not always be very accurate.

6. Text will not be hidden in a 3D model on the screen or on the plot when removing hidden lines. If you need to hide the text, you should place all of the text on a separate layer and **freeze** or turn the layer OFF before plotting.

7. 3D plot files are very large compared to others because the extents and all the entities of the drawing are based on the LIMITS of the WCS.

8. It is difficult and frustrating to try to plot multiple views of the same 3D object. You may have to run the paper through the plotter several times or copy the object on the screen to another location and manipulate the objects or change your viewpoint and then plot.

9. You cannot plot multiple viewports with AutoCAD Release 10.

10. There is no way to edit a 3D plot file.

PRODUCING HARD COPY AUTOSHADE IMAGES

To send a shaded image created with AutoSHADE to paper you must first make sure that AutoSHADE has been configured properly. To check the configuration of AutoSHADE start the AutoSHADE program by typing **SHADE** at the DOS prompt. From the **AutoSHADE interactive screen** select **Display** from the top of the screen. Look down at the pull-down window and see if the **Hard Copy** command is **grayed out**. If it is, then you will need to reconfigure AutoSHADE.

To reconfigure AutoSHADE exit the AutoSHADE interactive screen and from the DOS prompt delete the **SHADE.CFG** file. Then type **SHADE** to reconfigure AutoSHADE; it will ask you for the hardware configurations again. Answer all the questions as you did in the beginning of Chap. 7 when starting

AutoSHADE. Make sure to select the correct **hard copy device (postscript device)** when prompted.

After answering all the questions, you will be at the AutoSHADE interactive screen again.

Once AutoSHADE is reconfigured, you will notice that when you select **Display** from the top of the screen, the **Hard copy** command is no longer grayed out. If a command is grayed out in any of the pull-down windows within AutoSHADE, it means that the command is not available for you to use at this time.

To plot a shaded image follow the procedure below:

1. Select **File** from the top of the AutoSHADE interactive screen.

2. Scroll down the pull-down window and select **Open** or press **[F10]**.

3. From the **Select filmroll file** dialogue box select the FILMROLL required to view or plot. Then select **OK**.

4. Select a scene from the **Select Scene** dialogue box if requested. Then select **OK**.

5. Select **Display** from the top of the screen, then select FULL SHADE or press **[F4]**.

6. If the shaded image is at the desired position with the correct shading factors set, continue with the next step. If it is not, make the changes to the screen image before you plot.

7. Select **Display** from the top of the screen, then select **Hard copy** or press the **[ALT]** key in conjunction with **[F2]** function key. A checkmark appears in front of the option **Hard Copy**.

8. Now select **Display** from the top of the screen again, then select **FULL SHADE** or press **[F4]**.

9. The **Create Postscript output file** dialogue box will appear. Move the arrow pointer to the box which indicates the name of file and change it if desired then press **[ENTER]**. Then select OK at the bottom of the dialogue box. No extension is needed for the filename. The file resides in the current directory.

10. Quit AutoSHADE, and check to see if the postscript files (files with .PS extension) were created in the correct directory by typing: **DIR *.PS**

Now use the DOS print command to plot or print the rendered images. From the DOS prompt type **PRINT FILENAME.PS** and press **[ENTER]**. The printer must be configured to produce postscript files and AutoSHADE must be configured to use a postscript printer.

11. Make sure **Hard Copy** is turned OFF when you are finished plotting. When a checkmark is displayed in front of the **Hard Copy command in the Display** pull-down window, the **Hard copy** mode is **ON**. When it is not, it is **OFF**.

☞ **NOTE:** Make sure that **Record** mode is **OFF** before attempting to plot or print. **Record** mode is automatically grayed out when **Hard Copy** is selected and turned ON. **Hard Copy** mode is grayed out when **Record** mode is selected and turned ON.

SUMMARY

Now that you have used all of the AutoCAD 3D commands to draw, shade, and plot in 3D, you should feel confident enough to try designing your own models.

As with anything, you will need to practice what you have learned. Chapter 9 has several sample exercises for you to try. Take your time with each of the exercises and follow them step by step. If you are unsure about any of the procedures, review the chapter about that particular command and then continue.

There are also some optional problems in **App. A**. These are much more difficult and will require some planning before you start. Good luck and have fun.

CHAPTER NINE

3D MODELING EXERCISES

N ow that you have all the tools needed to work with AutoCAD in 3D, you will need to practice what you have learned. The following pages contain sample exercise drawings for you to try. Each of the exercises has been designed for you to apply all the AutoCAD 3D commands.

The exercises will give you practice in developing User Coordinate Systems; creating 3D meshes with the RULESURF, TABSURF, REVSURF, and EDGESURF commands; and using the AutoCAD 3D display commands to change your viewpoint.

Make sure to use separate layers whenever possible. All text should be placed on a separate layer. Remember to change back to the World Coordinate System before plotting.

MODEL EXERCISE 1: REVSURF COMMAND

Follow the procedure outlined here to create the goblet shown in Fig. 9-2.

1. Load AutoCAD. From the AutoCAD main menu select **1, Begin a NEW drawing.** Name the drawing anything you like.

2. Once inside the drawing editor turn the **GRIDS ON.** Enter the VPOINT command and change your viewpoint to a viewpoint of 1,-1,1 (type **VPOINT,** then **1,-1,1**).

3. Enter the **UCS** command and define a new User Coordinate System rotated **90** degrees around the **X** axis (type UCS, then X, then 90). This places the new defined UCS at a 90 degree angle from the World Coordinate System (WCS).

4. Select **Settings** from the pull-down windows, then select **Entity Creation....** Change the **color** to **red.** Turn **ORTHO** and **COORDS ON.**

5. Draw a vertical line about 10 inches long down the center of the screen (somewhere in the middle of the screen). Select **Settings** from the pull-down windows, then select **Entity Creation....** Change the **color** to **cyan.** Turn **ORTHO OFF.** Draw the polyline with the **PLINE** command just to the left of the red line as shown (Fig. 9-1).

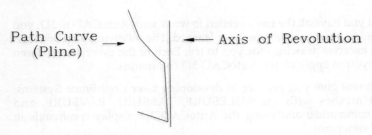

Path Curve ⟶   ⟵ Axis of Revolution
(Pline)

Figure 9-1 Line and polyline.

6. Enter the **PEDIT** command and select the polyline on the left as the object to edit. Use the **Spline curve** option within the **PEDIT** command to produce a smooth polyline. Exit the **PEDIT** command.

7. Enter the **REVSURF** command. Select the polyline on the left as the "**path curve**". Select the line as the "**axis of revolution.**" Use the default start and end angles for the revolution of the mesh in the **REVSURF** command. The mesh is revolved around the axis line.

8. Undo the last command with the **U** command. Select **3D** from the screen menu on the right. Now set the system variables **SURFTAB1** and **SURFTAB2** to equal **20**. Then try the **REVSURF** command again the same way you just did. **ERASE** the red axis line. The **goblet** should look similar to the one shown here (Fig. 9-2):

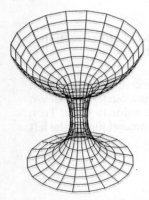

Figure 9-2 Goblet (REVSURF command).

MODEL EXERCISE 2: REVSURF COMMAND

1. Load AutoCAD. From the AutoCAD main menu select **1, Begin a NEW drawing**. Name the drawing anything you like.

2. Once inside the drawing editor turn the **GRIDS ON**. Enter the VPOINT command and change your viewpoint to a viewpoint of 1,-1,1 (type **VPOINT**, then **1,-1,1**). The VPOINT command can be accessed from the pull-down windows to give the same view by picking **Display** from the top of the screen, then **Vpoint 3D....**, then picking the box in the lower right corner of the VPOINT 3D dialogue box with an angle of 30 degrees above the X-Y plane.

3. Select **Settings** from the pull-down windows, then select **Entity Creation....** Change the **color** to **red**.

4. Enter the **UCS** command and define a new User Coordinate System rotated **90 degrees** around the **X** axis (type UCS, then X, then 90). This places the new defined UCS at a 90 degree angle from the World Coordinate System (WCS).

5. Draw a vertical line about 10 inches long down the center of the screen. Use **ORTHO** to keep the line straight. Select **Settings** from the pull-down windows then select **Entity Creation....** Change the **color** to **cyan**.

6. Draw the polyline with the **PLINE** command from the top end (use the ENDpoint OSNAP) of the line you just drew to form the polyline shown (Fig. 9-3). Turn **ORTHO OFF**.

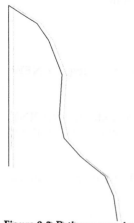

Figure 9-3 Path curve and axis of revolution.

7. Enter the **PEDIT** command and select the polyline on the left as the object to edit. Use the **Spline curve** option within the **PEDIT** command to produce a smooth polyline. Exit the **PEDIT** command.

8. Select **3D** from the screen menu at the right. Set the system variables **SURFTAB1** and **SURFTAB2** to equal **20**.

9. Enter the **REVSURF** command. Select the polyline on the right as the **"path curve."** Select the red line as the **"axis of revolution."** Use the default start and end angles for the revolution of the mesh in the **REVSURF** command. The mesh is revolved around the axis line (Fig. 9-4). **ERASE** the red line.

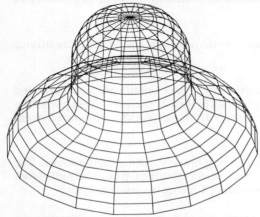

Figure 9-4 Bell-shaped mesh (REVSURF command).

The HIDE command can be used to remove the hidden lines. Make sure to change back to the World Coordinate System before plotting.

MODEL EXERCISE 3 : REVSURF COMMAND

1. Load AutoCAD. From the AutoCAD main menu select **1, Begin a NEW drawing**. Name the drawing anything you like.

2. Once inside the drawing editor turn the **GRIDS ON**. Enter the VPOINT command and change your viewpoint to a viewpoint of 1,-1,1 (type **VPOINT**, then **1,-1,1**).

3. Select **Settings** from the pull-down windows then select **Entity Creation....** Change the **color** to **red**.

4. Enter the **UCS** command and define a new User Coordinate System rotated **90** degrees around the **X** axis (type UCS, then X, then 90). This places the new defined UCS at a 90 degree angle from the World Coordinate System (WCS).

5. Turn **ORTHO ON**. Draw a horizontal line about 10 inches long in the center of the screen (Fig. 9-5). Select **Settings** from the pull-down windows, then select **Entity Creation....** Change the **color** to **cyan**. Turn **ORTHO OFF**.

6. Enter the **PLINE** command and draw the polyline command shown below (Fig. 9-5):

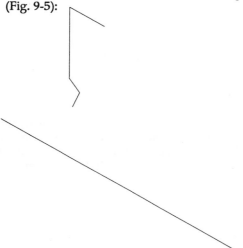

Figure 9-5 Path curve and axis of revolution.

7. **MIRROR** the polyline so that it looks like the one in Fig. 9-6. Turn **ORTHO ON** when picking the two points on the mirror line. Use an **End point** OSNAP to use the top of the line as the first point of the mirror line and do **not** delete the old object.

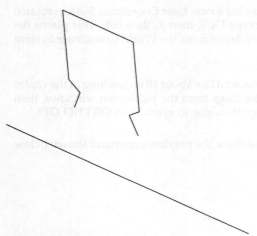

Figure 9-6 Mirrored polyline.

8. Enter the **PEDIT** command and select one of the polylines as the object to edit. Use the **Join** option in **PEDIT** to connect the two polylines together (pick both polylines). Use the **Spline curve** option within the **PEDIT** command to produce one smooth polyline. Exit the **PEDIT** command (Fig. 9-7).

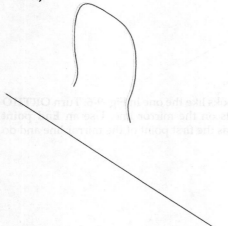

Figure 9-7 Path curve and axis of revolution.

9. Select **3D** from the screen menu on the right. Set the system variables **SURFTAB1** and **SURFTAB2** to equal 20.

10. Enter the **REVSURF** command. Select the new polyline as the **"path curve."** Select the red horizontal line as the **"axis of revolution."** Use the default start and end angles for the revolution of the mesh in the **REVSURF** command. The mesh is revolved around the axis line (Fig. 9-8). **ERASE** the red line. Use the **HIDE** command for hidden line removal. You may need to reduce the display of the drawing with the ZOOM command. Type ZOOM, then .7x.

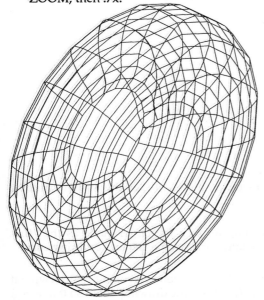

Figure 9-8 Tire-shaped mesh (REVSURF command).

11. Remember to change back to the World Coordinate System (WCS) before plotting.

MODEL EXERCISE 4 : RULESURF AND TABSURF COMMANDS

1. Load AutoCAD. From the AutoCAD main menu select **1, Begin a NEW drawing.** Name the drawing anything you like.

2. Once inside the drawing editor turn the **GRIDS ON.** Draw two circles with the same center point near the center of the screen, one with a **radius** of **1 inch** and the other with a **radius** of **.75 inch.**

3. Draw an eight sided polygon with a radius of 1 inch circumscribed about the larger circle with the same center point as the two circles (Fig. 9-9).

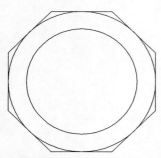

Figure 9-9 Drawing a nut.

4. Select **3D** from the screen menu at the right. Set the system variable **SURFTAB1** to equal **25**.

5. Enter the **RULESURF** command and pick the larger circle as the **"first defining curve"** and pick the smaller circle as the **"second defining curve"**.

6. Enter the **VPOINT** command and change your viewpoint to a viewpoint of 1,-1,1 (type **VPOINT**, then **1,-1,1**). **PAN** the drawing down so that it is at the bottom of the screen if necessary.

7. Enter the **COPY** command and copy the entire object 1 inch up in the **Z axis** (Fig. 9-10). Use a **window** to select the entire object and use the center point of the circle as the base point to copy from (use the CENter OSNAP tool). For **"second point of displacement"** type **@0,0,1**.

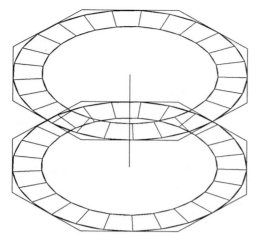

Figure 9-10 Copying the object in the Z axis.

8. Draw a line from the center point of the top circles to the center point of the bottom circles (use the CENter OSNAP tool).

9. Enter the **TABSURF** command and select the bottom octagon as the **"path curve"** and select the line (near the bottom endpoint) as the **"direction vector"** (Fig. 9-11).

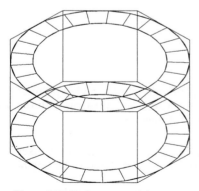

Figure 9-11 Path curve and direction vector.

10. ERASE the line in the middle. Use the **HIDE** command for hidden line removal. Reduce the drawing with the ZOOM command (type ZOOM, then .75).

MODEL EXERCISE 5: EDGESURF COMMAND

1. Load AutoCAD. From the AutoCAD main menu select **1, Begin a NEW drawing.** Name the drawing anything you like.

2. Once inside the drawing editor set the **GRID** and **SNAP** to .5. Turn both **GRID** and **SNAP ON.** Turn **COORDINATES [F6] ON** also.

3. Draw a 5- by 7-inch rectangle with the **LINE** command as shown below (Fig. 9-12).

Figure 9-12 5-by 7-inch rectangle.

4. Enter the VPOINT command and change your viewpoint to a viewpoint of 1,-1,1 (type **VPOINT**, then 1,-1,1). Reduce the size of the drawing with the **ZOOM** command to half the size (type ZOOM, then .5X).

5. Enter the **UCS** command and use the **Entity** option to define a new User Coordinate System with its origin at the lower left corner (pick the line at the bottom) of the rectangle (Fig. 9-13).

6. Reenter the UCS command to rotate the new **UCS** 90 degrees on its X axis as shown (type UCS, then X, then 90) (Fig. 9-13).

7. Enter the **UCSICON** command and use the **Origin** option to move the UCS icon to its new origin location at the bottom left corner of the rectangle as shown in Fig. 9-13 (type UCSICON, then OR).

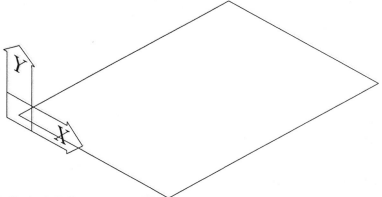

Figure 9-13 Creating a new UCS.

8. Draw lines from the bottom left corner of the rectangle (use the ENDpoint OSNAP and pick the endpoint of the bottom line to start) up in the **Y** axis using the **LINE** command as follows (see Fig. 9-14):

❖ **Command:**LINE
   From point:

Use the ENDpoint OSNAP and pick the lower left corner of the rectangle as a start point.

To point: **@0,5**
To point: **@-1.5,0**
To point: **@0,.5**
To point:. **X**
of   use the MIDpoint OSNAP tool to pick the midpoint of the bottom line.

(need YZ):   pick a point at about 30 degrees above the last point (use the coordinate display).

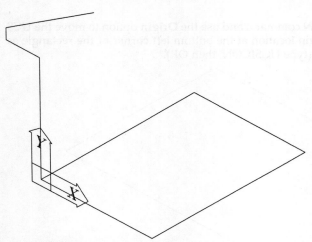

Figure 9-14 Drawing on the new UCS.

9. Exit the LINE command and mirror the four lines you just drew around the **Y** axis to complete the front view (Fig. 9-15). Use the very top endpoint of the top angled line as the first point on the mirror line and then turn **ORTHO ON** and pick anywhere down near the bottom of the screen for the second point on the mirror line. Do **not** delete the old object.

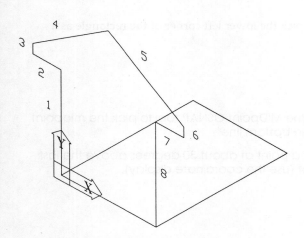

Figure 9-15 Completing the front view.

10. Enter the **PEDIT** command and join all eight lines together for the front view to make one single polyline from one side to the other. To do so enter the **PEDIT** command, pick location 1, then press **[ENTER]**. Make sure to answer **yes** when AutoCAD asks if you want to turn the line into a polyline. Then use the **Join** option within the **PEDIT** command and pick the other seven lines. Exit the PEDIT command.

11. **COPY** the new polyline in the front view to the back of the rectangle (Fig. 9-16). Make sure to use the ENDpoint OSNAP to grab the endpoints when copying. Turn **ORTHO OFF**. You may have to reduce the display of the drawing with the ZOOM command.

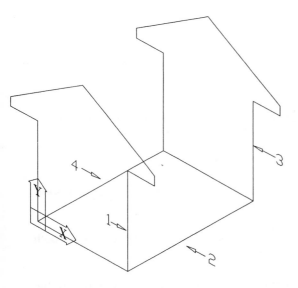

Figure 9-16 Completing the back view.

12. Select **3D** from the screen menu on the right. Set the system variables **SURFTAB1** and **SURFTAB2** to equal **40**.

13. Enter the **EDGESURF** command and pick the four lines at the points indicated as shown (Fig. 9-16) for edges 1, 2, 3, and 4. Notice the mesh which is created with the **EDGESURF** command (Fig. 9-17).

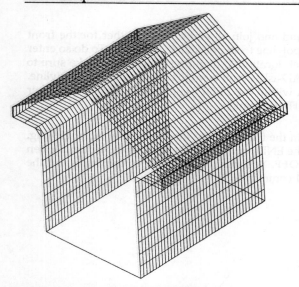

Figure 9-17 3DMESH using EDGESURF.

☞ NOTE: Don't try the HIDE command; it may take a very long time.

MODEL EXERCISE 6

1. Load AutoCAD. From the AutoCAD main menu select **1, Begin a NEW drawing**. Name the drawing anything you like.

2. Once inside the drawing editor set the **GRID** and **SNAP** to .5. Turn both **GRID** and **SNAP ON**.

3. Draw a 9- by 5-inch rectangle in the World Coordinate System. Use the CHANGE command to change the thickness of the rectangle to **5**.

4. Change your viewpoint with the VPOINT command to a viewpoint of 1,-1,1 (type **VPOINT**, then 1,-1,1). Reduce the display of the drawing with the ZOOM command (type ZOOM, then .7X).

5. Create the User Coordinate Systems shown below with the **UCS** command (Fig. 9-18). Use the UCS **3Point** option with the INTersection OSNAPS to locate the UCSs at each of the corners shown.

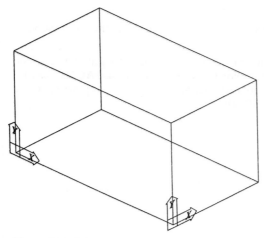

Figure 9-18 Creating a new UCS.

Save the two User Coordinate Systems as you create them with the **UCS Save** option. Use the names "FRONT" and "RIGHT" as the UCS names.

☞ **NOTE:** You will need to use the **UCSICON** command with the **Origin** option to move the UCS icon to its new origin location.

6. Create a new layer called **"MODEL."** Assign a color of green to layer model and set the layer current. Set the GRID and SNAP to .5.

7. Make the **FRONT** UCS active and draw the front view (six lines) in the **FRONT** UCS and copy the front side to the back side as shown below (Fig. 9-19).

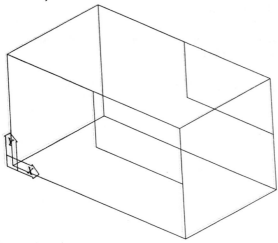

Figure 9-19 Drawing the front and back views.

☞ **NOTE:** Use the dimensions shown in Fig. 9-21 to draw the front view.

8. Freeze layer 0. Select **3D** from the screen menu at the right. Then select **3DFACE.** Use a running ENDpoint OSNAP to draw **3DFACES** (six) to connect all the corners of the front and back sides. Use the four points shown here for the first **3DFACE** (Fig. 9-20).

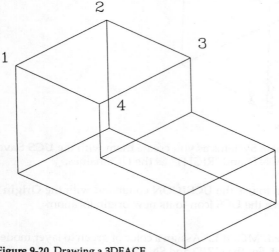

Figure 9-20 Drawing a 3DFACE.

9. Set the World Coordinate System as current. Type **UCS,** then **W,** then **[ENTER].** Draw a **3point** arc in the FRONT view (any size). Assign a thickness of 3 inches to the arc with the **CHANGE** command. Connect the top endpoints of the arc with a line (Fig. 9-21).

10. Make the **RIGHT UCS** current. Draw a circle in the center of the side view with a diameter of 2 inches and a thickness of 3 inches.

11. Use the **HIDE** command to remove the hidden lines (Fig. 9-21).

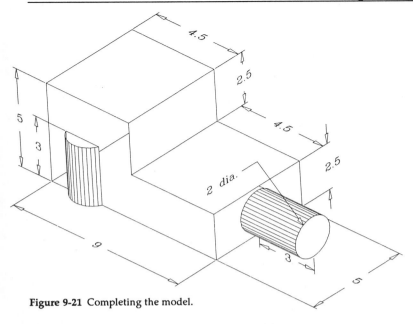

Figure 9-21 Completing the model.

12. Dimension the model as shown (Fig. 9-21).

MODEL EXERCISE 7

1. Load AutoCAD. From the AutoCAD main menu select **1, Begin a NEW drawing**. Name the drawing anything you like.

2. Once inside the drawing editor set the **GRID** and **SNAP** to **.5**. Turn both **GRID** and **SNAP ON**.

3. Draw a 3.5-inch square in the World Coordinate System. Use the CHANGE command to change the thickness of the square to 2.

4. Change your viewpoint with the VPOINT command to a viewpoint of 1,-1,1 (type **VPOINT**, then **1,-1,1**). Reduce the display of the drawing (Fig. 9-22) with the **ZOOM** command (type ZOOM, then .7X).

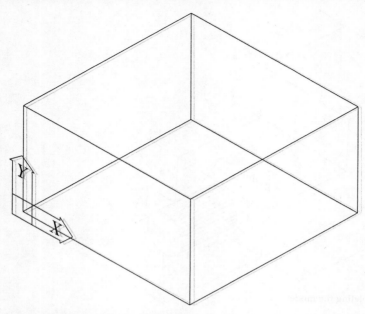

Figure 9-22 Creating the boundaries and UCS.

5. Create a new User Coordinate System in the FRONT view with the UCS **3Point** option. Use the INTersection OSNAP tool. Save the UCS with the UCS **Save** option and give it the name "FRONT."

6. Use the **UCSICON** command with the **ORIGIN** option to move the UCS icon to its new origin location at the lower left corner of the box (Fig. 9-22).

7. Create a new layer called "MODEL." Assign the color of **cyan** to the layer model and set it current.

8. Draw the FRONT view as shown (Fig. 9-23). Create a 3DFACE with the **3DFACE** command using the four points in the FRONT view (Fig. 9-23).

9. Copy the 3DFACE in the FRONT view to the BACK view. Use an INTersection OSNAP tool for the base point to copy from.

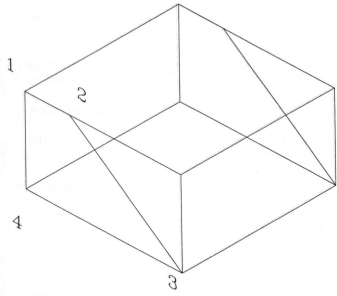

Figure 9-23 Drawing a 3DFACE.

10. Freeze layer 0. Use the four points shown below (Fig. 9-24) to draw a 3DFACE on the top of the model. Draw 3DFACES all around the model with the 3DFACE command to complete the figure.

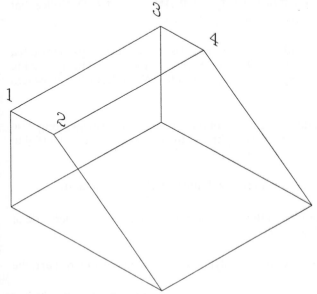

Figure 9-24 Completed model.

☞   **NOTE:** Use a running ENDpoint OSNAP tool to capture endpoints for all 3FACES (six).

11. Create a User Coordinate System (UCS) using the **3Point** option on the inclined surface with the origin located at the lower left corner of the surface

12. Draw a circle with a diameter of 3 inches in the center of the inclined surface.

13. Copy the circle 1 inch up in the **Z axis** on the inclined surface. Use the COPY command and use the value @0,0,1.

14. Use the **RULESURF** command to connect the two circles with a mesh.

☞   **NOTE:** The **SURFTAB1** system variable should be set to **25** before using the **RULESURF** command.

MODEL EXERCISE 8

1. Load AutoCAD. From the AutoCAD main menu select **1, Begin a NEW drawing.** Name the drawing "MUG."

2. Once inside the drawing editor set the **GRID** and **SNAP** to .5. Turn both **GRID** and **SNAP ON.** Enter the VPOINT command and change your viewpoint to a viewpoint of 1,-1,1 (type **VPOINT**, then **1,-1,1**). Notice that the GRID boundaries determine the paper size.

3. Enter the **UCS** command and define a new User Coordinate System rotated **90** degrees around the **X** axis (type UCS, then X, then 90). This places the new defined UCS at a 90 degree angle from the World Coordinate System (WCS).

4. Draw a vertical line down the center of the screen about 10 inches long. Use **ORTHO [F8]** to keep the line straight and turn the coordinates ON **[F6]** to determine the length of the line.

5. Change the color of the line to **red** with the **CHANGE** command.

6. Draw a polyline from the bottom endpoint of the red line to the left side of the line as shown (Fig. 9-25).

7. FILLET the bottom corner of the polyline with a radius of 1 inch. Turn the **GRIDS OFF.**

Figure 9-25 Path curve and axis of revolution.

☞ **NOTE:** Set **SURFTAB1** and **SURFTAB2** equal to 20.

8. Enter the **REVSURF** command and pick the polyline on the left as the **"path curve"** and the red line as the **"axis of revolution."** Use the default start and end angles (0 and 360) to produce the revolution (Fig. 9-26). **ERASE** the red axis line.

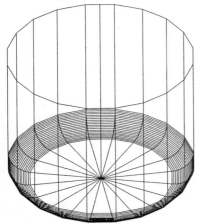

Figure 9-26 3DMESH (mug).

9. Draw a polyline with the **PLINE** command for the handle of the mug similar to the one shown in Fig. 9-27. Draw the polyline away from the object and move it into place afterward.

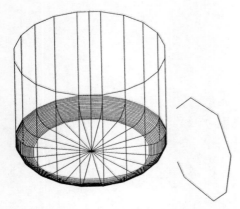

Figure 9-27 Drawing the handle with PLINE.

10. Use the **PEDIT** command to smooth out the polyline with the **Fit curve** option.

11. Use the **OFFSET** command to offset the polyline as shown (Fig. 9-28). Use an offset distance of **.25**.

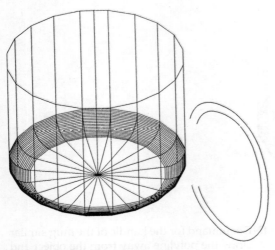

Figure 9-28 Completing the handle.

12. Use the **CHANGE** command to change the **thickness** of both polylines to .5.

13. Move the handle into place with the **MOVE** command and the **object snaps** (Fig. 9-29). Use the OSNAP ENDpoint tool for selecting the base point of the lower part of the handle. Move the handle into the mug using the NEArest OSNAP tool to select one of the extruded lines on the mug.

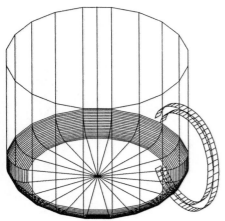

Figure 9-29 3DMESH of a mug.

13. Move the handle into place with the MOVE command and the object snaps (Fig. 9-29). Use the OSNAP ENDpoint tool to select the base point of the lower part of the handle. Move the handle into the mug using the NEArest OSNAP tool to select one of the extruded lines on the mug.

Figure 9-27 3DMESH of a mug.

OPTIONAL PROBLEMS

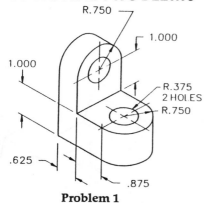

Problem 1

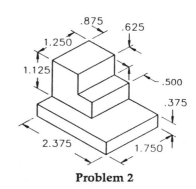

Problem 2

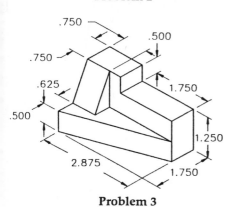

Problem 3

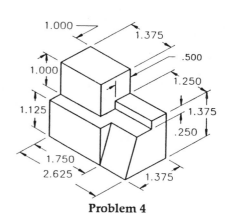

Problem 4

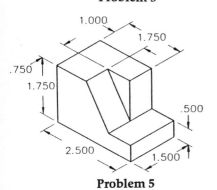

Problem 5

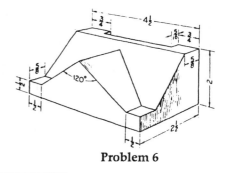

Problem 6

Problems 6, 11-13 and 20-25 were reprinted from "Engineering Drawing & Graphic Technology", French/Vierck, McGraw-Hill, © 1978.

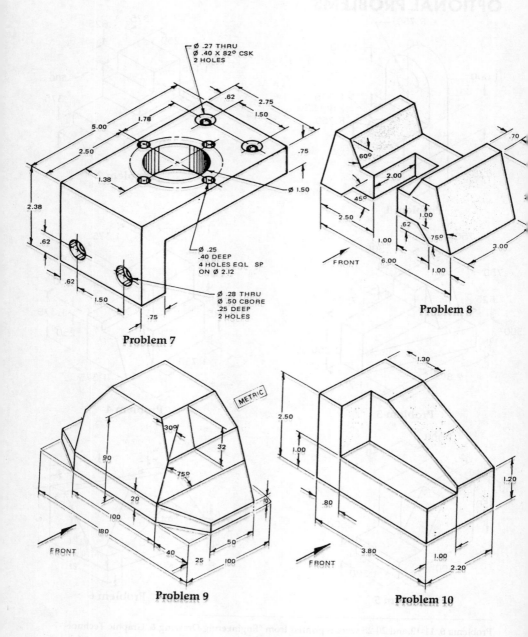

Ø .27 THRU
Ø .40 X 82° CSK
2 HOLES

.62   2.75

1.78   1.50

5.00

2.50   .75

1.38   Ø 1.50

2.38

.62

.62   Ø .25
.40 DEEP
4 HOLES EQL SP
ON Ø 2.12

1.50

.75   Ø .28 THRU
Ø .50 CBORE
.25 DEEP
2 HOLES

Problem 7

.70

60°

2.00

45°

2.50   1.00

1.00   .62   75°   3.00

FRONT

6.00   1.00

Problem 8

METRIC

30°

90   32

75°

20

100   10

180

40   25   50

100

FRONT

Problem 9

1.30

2.50

1.00   1.20

.80

3.80   1.00

2.20

FRONT

Problem 10

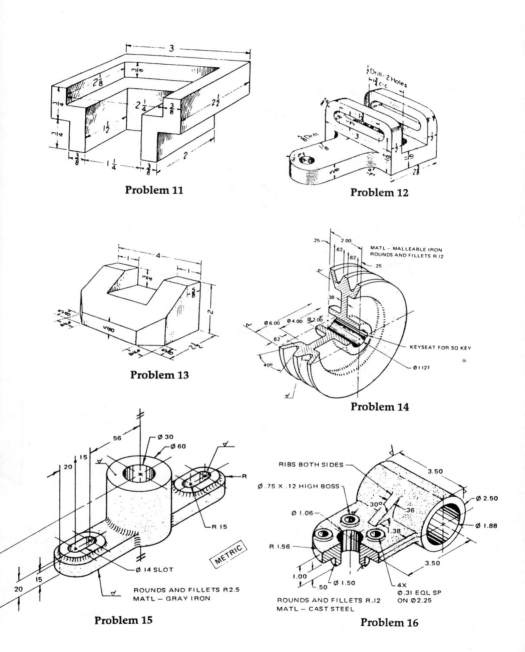

Problem 11

Problem 12

Problem 13

Problem 14

Problem 15

Problem 16

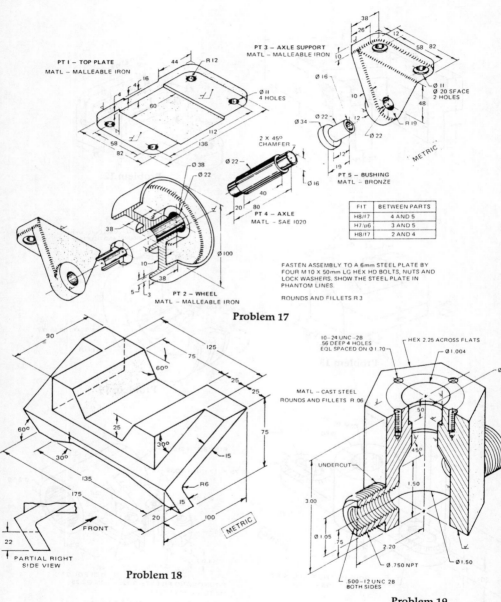

PT I – TOP PLATE
MATL – MALLEABLE IRON

44   R 12

16
4   4
60
112
58
82
136

Ø 11
4 HOLES

PT 3 – AXLE SUPPORT
MATL – MALLEABLE IRON

38
26
12
58   82
10

Ø 16

10

Ø 11
Ø 20 SFACE
2 HOLES

48

R 19

Ø 34   Ø 22
12
Ø 22

METRIC

2 X 45°
CHAMFER

Ø 22

Ø 38
Ø 22

Ø 22

40
20   80

PT 4 – AXLE
MATL – SAE 1020

Ø 16

12
19

PT 5 – BUSHING
MATL – BRONZE

38

10

38

5

Ø 100

PT 2 – WHEEL
MATL – MALLEABLE IRON

FIT	BETWEEN PARTS
H8/f7	4 AND 5
H7/p6	3 AND 5
H8/f7	2 AND 4

FASTEN ASSEMBLY TO A 6mm STEEL PLATE BY
FOUR M 10 X 50mm LG HEX HD BOLTS, NUTS AND
LOCK WASHERS. SHOW THE STEEL PLATE IN
PHANTOM LINES.

ROUNDS AND FILLETS R 3

Problem 17

90
125
75
60°
25
25

60°
25
30°
75
15

60°
30°
135
175
R 6
15
20   100

METRIC

FRONT

22
PARTIAL RIGHT
SIDE VIEW

Problem 18

10–24 UNC –2B
.56 DEEP 4 HOLES
EQL SPACED ON Ø 1.70

HEX 2.25 ACROSS FLATS
Ø 1.004

Ø

MATL – CAST STEEL
ROUNDS AND FILLETS R .06

50

45°

UNDERCUT

1.50

3.00

.75

Ø 1.05

2.20

Ø .750 NPT

Ø .1.50

.500–12 UNC 2B
BOTH SIDES

Problem 19

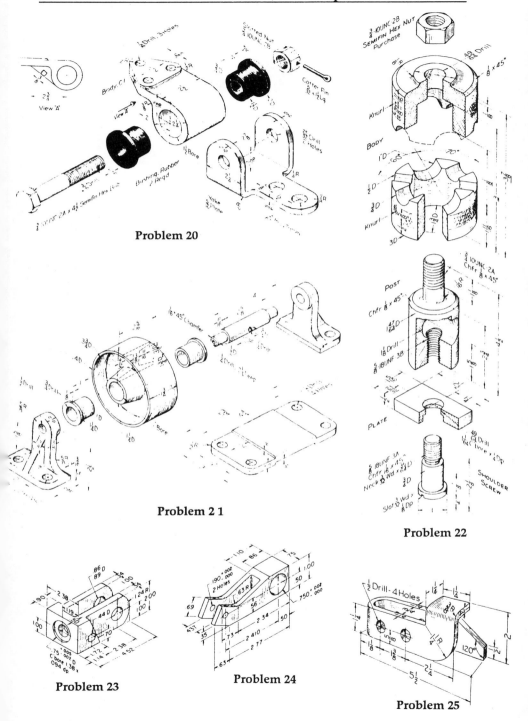

Problem 20

Problem 2 1

Problem 22

Problem 23

Problem 24

Problem 25

GLOSSARY

AXES

Imaginary lines to describe the X, Y, and Z directions when viewing an object in the AutoCAD drawing editor.

BEZIER MESH

A three-dimensional mesh which is generated by editing a mesh created originally with the 3DMESH, EDGESURF, or REVSURF commands. The smooth bezier mesh will resemble the original mesh but will not pass through the same points as the original mesh.

BROKEN PENCIL ICON

Picture of a broken pencil which is displayed at the lower left corner of the screen or viewport. The broken pencil icon indicates that the viewpoint you are looking at is not parallel to the current UCS. Therefore you should not draw from that viewpoint.

CLIPPING PLANES

Imaginary planes used to cut off sections of your drawing so as to look inside of a three-dimensional model. The DVIEW command **Clip** option is used to activate the clipping planes.

CUBIC MESH

A three-dimensional mesh which is generated by editing a mesh created originally with the 3DMESH, EDGESURF, or REVSURF commands. The cubic mesh approximates a number of control points which are slightly different from the original mesh.

DIALOGUE BOX

A box which appears on the screen which allows you to access the AutoCAD command and its options such as the HATCH command.

DVIEWBLOCK HOUSE

An AutoCAD file which is displayed when using the DVIEW command to orientate the display of the drawing. The DVIEWBLOCK house is a picture of a house. Your drawing will be rotated to the same orientation as the orientation of the house when exiting the DVIEW command.

ELEVATION

The **elevation** of an entity in the drawing defines its starting point above or below the X-Y plane.

EXTRUSION

The thickness or height property given to an AutoCAD entity. The direction of the extrusion is perpendicular to the X-Y plane.

FILTERS

A point can be specified by designating several intermediate points and forming a final point from selected X, Y, and Z coordinates. The AutoCAD filters are especially useful for extracting points from existing entities of an object.

HARD COPY

A paper printout of the drawing generated from the computer.

ICON

A graphical symbol on the screen or template used to simply describe and access a command.

MESH

A **mesh** is a single entity that attempts to place **multiple 3DFACES** on the surface of an object. A mesh is defined by a simple matrix of M and N vertices. A good analogy would be to view the mesh as a grid system with columns and rows. The M and N values specify the position of the vertices for the columns and rows.

ORIGIN

X, Y, and Z coordinates of (0,0,0) given to a point on a drawing to define the X, Y, and Z intersection point.

PERSPECTIVE MODE

An option within the DVIEW command used to orientate the display of the drawing so that it appears in perspective. It simulates a distance with parallel lines converging to a single vanishing point.

QUADRATIC MESH

A three-dimensional mesh which is generated by editing a mesh created originally with the 3DMESH, EDGESURF, or REVSURF commands. The smooth quadratic mesh will resemble the original mesh but will not pass through the exact same points as the original mesh.

RIGHT HAND RULE

Using your hand to define all coordinate systems used in a drawing. Place your right hand near the screen with your palm facing you. Extend your thumb in the direction of the positive X axis and point your index finger toward the positive Y axis. Bend your other fingers down slightly to indicate the positive direction of the Z axis.

SCROLL BAR

Horizontal and vertical bars which are displayed in the drawing editor when using the DVIEW command to rotate the display on the screen.

SOLID MODELS

Solid models are 3D types of models that look much like shaded surface models but have additional properties. Solid models define the space a real object would occupy. Solid models can have properties such as **weight, volume, mass,** and **density.**

SURFACE MODELS

Surface models are similar to wireframe models except they can have the outside surfaces defined. A surface model is really a wireframe model with boundaries. Surface models can be used to show colors and shadows. These types of models are more clearly defined than wireframe models.

THICKNESS

Defines the height of an entity in the Z axis. The terms thickness and height are used interchangeably.

3D MODELS

A 3D drawing of an object which can be created and viewed numerous ways. **All 3D models have length, depth, and height (three dimensions).**

3D POLYLINES

A polyline drawn in three-dimensional space. All vertices of the polyline have different X, Y, and Z values.

TRUE 3D

A **true 3D drawing** or **model** is one which can be viewed from any angle or viewpoint to give a true representation of the model.

UCS DIALOGUE

A box which appears on the screen which allows you to access the UCS command options. To use the UCS dialogue box select SETTINGS from the pull-down windows at the top of the screen. Scroll down and select **UCS DIALOGUE....**

UDENSITY

An AutoCAD option which sets the **Surfu** system variable used to control the density of 3D wireframe cross-grid meshes.

UNITS

A distance defined by the user. The UNITS command is used to define the AutoCAD drawing units to work in. Examples of types of units are decimal, architectural, fractions, and engineering.

USER COORDINATE SYSTEM (UCS)

A movable user-defined coordinate system or plane in which to work. Similar to the AutoCAD World Coordinate System (WCS) except the user can define the origin location and the X and Y axes direction. The **UCS** command is used to define separate coordinate systems within a drawing. The **origin** (0,0) of the user-defined UCS can be located anywhere in the AutoCAD drawing editor. Several of these User Coordinate Systems may be defined and saved.

VDENSITY

An AutoCAD option which sets the **Surfv** system variable used to control the density of 3D wireframe cross-grid meshes.

VIEWPORTS

A section of the drawing editor which can display any view of an object. The screen can be split into up to four separate viewports. Drawing, panning, and zooming can be done in each viewport separately.

WCS ICON

A WCS icon is displayed in the **lower left corner** of the screen and is used to describe the World Coordinate System. A "**W**" in the icon indicates that you are currently working in the **World** Coordinate System. A "**+**" in the UCS icon indicates that you are currently working in a **user**-defined coordinate system. Whichever icon is displayed is considered the **current** coordinate system or **current UCS**. All coordinate input and displays will be relative to the current UCS.

WIREFRAME MODELS

Wireframe models are basic types of models composed of **lines** or **edges**. The lines used to describe the wireframe model are lines placed in three-dimensional space with the AutoCAD **LINE** command. There are no actual surfaces in the model.

WORLD COORDINATE SYSTEM

The World Coordinate System is defined as the **X-Y plane** or the cartesian coordinate system. It is similar to working with graph paper with **X** and **Y axes**. The X axis is the horizontal direction and the Y axis is the vertical direction. All points are located with an X and Y value in the form (X,Y). The center point, where the X and Y axes intersect is called the origin, indicated by (0,0).

WORLDVIEW

AutoCAD system variable to set the current coordinate system to the World Coordinate System (WCS).

X-Y PLANE

The cartesian coordinate system used to create all 2D drawings with AutoCAD. The X axis is horizontal and Y axis is vertical.

X-Y-Z COORDINATES

All coordinate systems also have a **Z axis** in addition to their **X** and **Y** axes to use for the third dimension of **height,** or **thickness.** The Z axis is defined by the right hand rule described earlier as perpendicular to the X-Y plane.

Z AXIS

Used to locate 3D points using (X,Y,Z) coordinate triple. The Z axis is perpendicular to the X-Y plane and represents the height, or thickness, of an object.

AUTOCAD 3D COMMAND REFERENCE

CHANGE COMMAND

Used to CHANGE an existing entity. To change the size of an entity or the location of one of its points or one or more of its properties. Properties are colors, linetypes, layers, elevation, and thickness. The command format is:

❖ **COMMAND**:CHANGE
Select objects:
pick objects, then **[ENTER]**
Properties/<Change point>:
type **P** to change a property or pick new point, then **[ENTER]**.
If you type **P**, the following prompt appears:
Change what Property (Color/Elev/LAyer/
LType/Thickness)?:

One of the properties can be changed here.

CHPROP COMMAND

The CHPROP **(Change properties)** command is the same as the CHANGE command except only the properties can be changed. The command format is:

❖ **Command**:CHPROP
Select objects:
pick objects to change, then **[ENTER]**
Change what property
(Color/Layer/Ltype/Thickness)?:

One of the properties can be changed by typing one of the above options.

DVIEW COMMAND

Used to dynamically orientate the display of the drawing on the screen. The DVIEW (Dynamic view) command is similar to the VPOINT command with more options. A **scroll bar** is displayed on the side of the screen first and then on the top to control the **CAMERA angle**. You can use the pointing device or type in values at the keyboard to dynamically rotate the object. The command format is:

❖ **Command**:DVIEW
Select objects:
Camera/TArget/Distance/POints/PAn/
Zoom/TWist/CLip/Hide/Off/Undo/<eXit>:

DVIEW command options and their functions are:

Camera	Used to set the CAMERA angle relative to the TARGET (selected objects)
Clip	Used to set the front and back clipping planes
Distance	Sets the distance between CAMERA and TARGET, also turns **perspective mode ON**
eXit	Exits the DVIEW command
Hide	Performs hidden line removal
Off	Turns **perspective mode OFF**
PAn	Pans selected objects across the screen dynamically
POints	Specifies CAMERA and TARGET points
TArget	Selects the TARGET angle relative to the CAMERA
TWist	Creates a view **Twist** angle
Undo	**Undoes** a DVIEW subcommand
Zoom	Dynamically ZOOMs in and out on selected objects

If you select **CLIP**, the following options are available:

Back	Sets the back clipping plane
Front	Sets the front clipping plane
Off	Turns clipping OFF

EDGESURF COMMAND

The **EDGESURF** command is used to create a mesh between **four** known **edges** or **sides. EDGESURF** means **edge-defined surface patch** and will draw a coons surface patch between four edges. The command format is:

❖ **Command:**EDGESURF
  Select edge 1:
  Select edge 2:
  Select edge 3:
  Select edge 4:

Select four separate edges. The system variables **SURFTAB1** and **SURFTAB2** are both used to control the density of the mesh created with EDGESURF.

ELEV (ELEVATION) COMMAND

The **ELEV**ation command is used to assign a base, or starting point for an entity in the X-Y-Z axis. It also sets the extrusion thickness for all subsequent entities drawn. The command format is:

❖ **Command:**ELEV
New current elevation:
New current thickness:
Enter value for the elevations and thicknesses of all entities to
be drawn.

GRID COMMAND

Used to set up the GRID increments in the drawing editor. The **[F7]** function
key toggles the GRID ON and OFF. The command format is:

❖ **Command:**GRID
Grid spacing (X) or ON/OFF/SNAP/Aspect<0'-0">:

HIDE COMMAND

The **HIDE** command is used to **remove hidden lines** in a drawing after
changing your viewpoint from 2D to 3D. The command format is:

❖ **Command:**HIDE
Regenerating drawing.
Removing hidden lines: 125

ISOPLANE COMMAND

Used to select the current isometric plane and corresponding axes to work in.
The ISOPLANES command places you on another plane in the drawing. The
ISOPLANE command allows only three planes in which to draw and their
origins cannot be moved. You can draw on the LEFT, TOP, or FRONT planes
by changing the direction of the X and Y axes. The command format is:

❖ **Command:**ISOPLANE
left/Top/Right/(Toggle):

If you press **[ENTER]**, AutoCAD will toggle you from the current plane to the
next, from LEFT to TOP to RIGHT.

[CTRL] and **[E]** keys used together will also toggle from the current plane to
the next.

LIMITS

The LIMITS command is used to set the drawing limits or paper size. The lower
left corner, or the drawing origin, is (0,0) and the upper right corner can be set
to any desired size. The AutoCAD default limits are 9 by 12 units.

❖ **Command:**LIMITS
ON/OFF/<Lower left corner> < *0'-0",0'-0"*>:
Upper right corner<*1'-0",0'-9"*>:

PEDIT COMMAND

PEDIT (Polyline edit) command can be used to edit 2D and 3D polylines. The command is used the same way as it is for 2D polylines. 3D polylines cannot have their line widths changed. The command format is:

❖ **Command:**PEDIT
Select polyline:
Select polyline.
Close/Edit vertex/Spline curve/Decurve/Undo/eXit<X>:

If you select **Edit vertex,** the PEDIT command issues a new set of options to choose to edit one of the polylines vertices.

Next/Previous/Break/Insert/Move/Regen/Straighten/eXit <N>:

PLAN COMMAND

The **PLAN** command is used to return to the **PLAN view** of the drawing (VPOINT 0,0,1). The PLAN view will only change the current UCS to its PLAN view.

❖ **Command:**PLAN
<Current UCS>/UCS/World:

The options are:

Current UCS	<default>This sets the display to the PLAN view of the current User Coordinate System.
UCS	This lets you set the display to the PLAN view of a previously saved UCS.
World	This sets the display to the PLAN view with respect the World Coordinate System.

REDRAWALL

This command will refresh the screen. Used to **REDRAW** all the viewports on the screen when set to multiple viewports with the VPORTS command. The command format is:

❖ **Command:**REDRAWALL

REGENALL

The **REGENALL** command will regenerate all the viewports on the screen. Regenerating a drawing with the REGENALL command will be much more time consuming with multiple viewports than using the REGEN command with a single viewport. The command format is:

❖ **Command:**REGENALL

REVSURF COMMAND

The **REVSURF** command is a more complex command and uses a grid-type mesh with both columns and rows. REVSURF means **surfaces of revolution**. The REVSURF command causes a mesh or surface to revolve around a fixed axis. The system variables **SURFTAB1** and **SURFTAB2** are both used to control the density of the mesh.

❖ **Command:**REVSURF
Select path curve:
pick a path curve
Select axis of revolution:
pick an axis line.
Start angle <0>:
press **[ENTER]**
Included angle (+=ccw, -=cw) <Full circle>:
press **[ENTER]**

You can specify the amount to revolve the object around the axis at the **Include angle** prompt. A value of **360** will produce a full revolution.

RULESURF COMMAND

The **RULESURF** (ruled surfaces) command is used to define a mesh or surface between two existing entities in a drawing. This is a single line mesh. The command format is:

❖ **Command:**RULESURF
Select first defining curve:
pick first curve
Select second defining curve:
pick second curve

SNAP COMMAND

Used to set the SNAP increment in the drawing editor. The command format is:

❖ **Command**:SNAP
Snap spacing(X) or ON/OFF/Aspect/Rotate/Style <0'-1">:

SETVAR COMMAND

The SETVAR command can also be used to change these system variables. They can be found under the 3D option in the root screen menu. To use the **SETVAR** command type SETVAR.

❖ **Command**:SETVAR
Variable name or ?:
type **SURFTAB1** or **SURFTAB2 [ENTER]**
New value for SURFTAB1 :
enter a value, then press **[ENTER]**

SURFTAB1

SURFTAB1 is an AutoCAD system variable which controls the density of a mesh created with the **RULESURF** and **TABSURF** commands. These are not actually cross-grids but single lines forming the mesh. SURFTAB1 controls the density of **single line meshes**. The command format is:

❖ **Command**:SETVAR
'SETVAR Variable name or ? <SURFTAB>1: SURFTAB1
New value for SURFTAB1 :

SURFTAB2

SURFTAB2 is an AutoCAD system variable which used together with SURFTAB1 controls the density of any **cross-grid mesh** as created with the **REVSURF** and **EDGESURF** commands. The command format is:

❖ **Command**:SETVAR
'SETVAR Variable name or ? <SURFTAB>2: SURFTAB2
New value for SURFTAB2 <15>:

TABSURF COMMAND

The **TABSURF** command (tabulated surfaces) requires one entity as a path curve and then a direction vector. The mesh or surface is extruded from the path curve selected relative to a direction and distance of another selected entity on the drawing. The command format is:

❖ **Command**:TABSURF
Select Path curve:
pick an entity

Select direction vector:
pick a direction vector

3DFACE COMMAND

The **3DFACE** command creates a **SOLID** surface on an object. The 3DFACE command is similar to the SOLID command. Points should be selected in a clockwise or counterclockwise direction. Use the Invisible option preceding the first point of that edge to make an edge of a 3DFACE invisible when viewed as a wireframe.

3DFACES are not solid filled. The HIDE command considers them to be transparent if they are planer. If they are nonplaner, HIDE draws a wireframe view. The command format is:

❖ **Command:**3DFACE
First point:
Second point:
Third point:
Fourth point:
press **[ENTER]** to exit

3DMESH COMMAND

The **3DMESH** command is used to create general polygon meshes which cannot be otherwise created with **RULESURF, TABSURF, REVSURF,** and **EDGESURF.** The **3DMESH** command can be used to create   **custom 3D meshes,** where you define the density and location of each vertex in the mesh. A defined **matrix** (cross-grid) size is required. You are prompted for the **M** and **N** size of the matrix where **M** is the number of vertices in one direction and **N** is the number of vertices in the other direction. The command format is:

❖ **Command:**3DMESH
Mesh M size:
enter a value, then **[ENTER]**
Mesh N size:
enter a value, then **[ENTER]**
Vertex (0,0):
Vertex (0,1):
Vertex (0,2):
Vertex (0,3):
Vertex (0,4):
   .
   .
   .

Pick points on the screen for each vertex to define the mesh. The mesh appears after all vertices have been picked.

3DPOLY COMMAND

The **3DPOLY** command creates a three-dimensional polyline consisting of all straight line segments in three-dimensional space. This command is very similar to the **PLINE** command. 3D polylines are polylines drawn from one plane to another or from one UCS to another. 3D polylines can be edited with the PEDIT command. The command format is:

❖ **Command:**3DPOLY
From point:
pick start point
Close/Undo/<Endpoint of Line>:
type **X,Y,Z values** for the succeeding points, then **[ENTER]**

The option **Close**, or **C**, within the **3DPOLY** command will close the polyline back to the starting point of the segment or polyline, providing you have more than one segment.

UCS COMMAND

Used to define a new User Coordinate System somewhere in the X-Y-Z axis. The coordinate system can have its own origin location and X, Y, and Z axes directions. The command format is:

❖ **Command:**UCS
Origin/Zaxis/3point/Entity/View/
X/Y/Z/Prev/Restore/Save/Del/?/<World>:

The UCS command options are:

O (Origin)	Defines a new UCS by establishing a new origin (X,Y,Z). The origin can be selected with the pointing device or typed at the keyboard. *Origin point <0,0,0>:*　　(enter new point)
ZA (ZAxis)	Defining a new Z axis angle. The X-Y plane will adjust perpendicular to the new plane.
3Point	Pick three points to define a new UCS and plane. The origin is selected, then the positive X direction, and then the positive Y direction.
E (Entity)	Defines a UCS by selecting an existing entity in a drawing. The new UCS is aligned with the selected entity with respect to the UCS in which the entity was created.
V (View)	Defines a new UCS which is parallel to your viewing direction. Sets X as horizontal and Y as vertical looking directly at the screen.
X/Y/Z	Rotates the current UCS around one of the axes.
P (Previous)	Restores the previously saved UCS.

R (Restore)	Restores a saved UCS by name.
S (Save)	Saves a UCS by name.
D (Delete)	Deletes a saved UCS.
?	Lists all saved UCS.
W (World)	Restores the World Coordinate System (**WCS**). This is the UCS command default.

UCSICON COMMAND

The UCSICON command controls the **display** of the UCS icons. It is used to position a new UCS icon on the drawing. The command format is:

❖ **Command:**UCSICON
   ON/OFF/All/Noorigin/ORigin/<Current ON/OFF state>:

The UCSICON command options are:

ON	Turns the UCS icon display **ON**
OFF	Turns the UCS icon display **OFF**
A (all)	Makes the changes to UCS icons active in all viewports
N	Always display the icon at the lower left corner of the viewport (Noorigin)
OR	Forces the icon to display at the origin of the current UCS

If the UCSs are set to appear at the their origin locations with the UCSICON command and the object does not fit on the screen, the UCS icon will appear at the lower left corner of the drawing editor or current viewport.

VIEW COMMAND

Used to save a screen display with a given name. The view can be used to save a zoomed up window or any rotation desired. The command format is:

❖ **Command:**VIEW
   ?/Delete/Restore/Save/Window:
   type **Save [ENTER]**
   View name to save:
   type a name, then **[ENTER]**

VPOINT COMMAND

Used to change your viewpoint when looking at an object on the screen. The command format is:

❖ **Command:**VPOINT
   Rotate/<viewpoint> <0.0000,0.0000,0.0000>:

The following options appear on the screen menu:

rotate	Allows you to rotate the object around a specified point (pivot point)
axes	Displays the AutoCAD X-Y-Z axes for orientating the display
plan	Returns to the current UCS PLAN view
HIDE	Performs hidden line removal

VPORTS COMMAND

The **VPORTS**, or viewports command, will split the screen into up to four screens. This gives you the opportunity to view a drawing several different ways at the same time. AutoCAD command operations can be done within each individual viewport. Different sections of a drawing can be displayed in different viewports at different angles. The command format is:

❖ **Command:**VPORTS
Save/Restore/Delete/Join/Single/?/2/<3>/4:

The options are:

S	Saves a viewport configuration with a name (You may want to use names such as VP1, VP2)
R	Restores a saved viewport configuration (Viewport configurations can be restored at any time and will reflect all changes made)
D	Deletes a saved viewport configuration
J	Joins one or more viewports together
SI	Restores to a single viewport screen
?	Lists the saved viewport configurations
2	Divides the current viewport into two viewports
3	Divides the current viewport into three viewports
4	Divides the current viewport into four viewports

ZOOM COMMAND

The ZOOM command is used to increase or decrease the display of the drawing in the drawing editor. The command format is:

❖ **Command:**ZOOM
All/Center/Dynamic/Extents/
Left/Prev/Window/<Scale(X)>:

Index

ABOUT THE AUTHOR

Frank J. Johnson is a CAD systems specialist with CADD Value Corporation, Fairfield, New Jersey, where he installs CAD systems and conducts AutoCAD training for corporate clients. His previous positions include CAD systems specialist with D. B. Technology, Inc., where he designed and conducted training courses in AutoCAD, 3D modeling, and AutoLISP; and systems engineer with Vista Computer Center, where he was responsible for coordinating LAN networks and CAD workstations.